THE COMPLETE GUIDE TO FISH TANK CARE AND MAINTENANCE

MYLES GOODWIN

COPYRIGHT

CONTENTS

1 FISH TANK VS. AQUARIUM – WHAT'S THE DIFFERENCE?

When it comes to connotation, the main difference between a fish tank and an aquarium is that the term "aquarium" has a more expensive, decorative implication while fish tank is more basic. According to the Cambridge dictionary, an aquarium is a glass container in which fish and other water creatures can be kept. On the other hand, a fish tank is a glass container used for keeping fish in, especially pet tropical fish. In many situations, "fish tank" and "aquarium" could be used interchangeably.

The phrase "My, what a beautiful _____" would more likely be completed with "aquarium" rather than "fish tank."

Also, if one says they have an aquarium in their house, the impression is usually of something much larger with elaborately decorated expensive, and often exotic tropical species with a seascape in aqua color lighting. A small, inexpensive setup easily obtained and maintained with a small amount of fish can be referred to as a "fish tank." Anything from a bowl up to the 15 to 20 gallon containers that you can easily cart out of the store under one arm can have the "fish tank" label.

Because of the sheer presence of the aquatic system, larger size tanks from 55 to 75 gallons will usually be labeled "aquariums." A large public aquatic zoo can rightfully be called an aquarium. A rectangle with 20 gallons of glass lined with water, a smattering of pebbles, and some goldfish is a 'fish tank.' An "aquarium" is a 20 gallon glass rectangle filled with water, a landscaped bed of gravel, decorations, plants and a variety of aquatic life selected with a sense of aquatic balance or to imitate a natural marine climate. You can call a fish tank an aquarium, but you cannot easily get away with calling an aquarium a fish tank. Think of it this way: you go to the aquarium with your family to look at many different fish tanks, but you do not go to the fish tank to look at many different aquariums.

From a different perspective, one might ask themselves the following questions:

1. "Can you pick it up by yourself when it is empty?" If the answer is "Yes", it is a fish tank; if the answer is "No", it is an aquarium.

2. A fish tank is a basic item; an aquarium has pebbles, weed, thermostats, air-feed, ornaments, etc. in it.

3. A fish tank that goes for $30 is cheaper than an aquarium of the same size and shape, which might cost $60.

4. Some fish at restaurants have a fish tank where you can choose the fish you want to eat. Fish from an aquarium is not eaten.

Some would say that a tank is a vessel for containing animals and their environment, while an aquarium is a public institution that exhibits those animals for education or entertainment. At the end of the day, the language can often be inconsistent and interchangeable, but both terms typically paint similar pictures.

2 10 EASY STEPS TO MAINTAINING A FISH TANK

Keeping your fish healthy usually has two parts. The first is feeding, and the second is aquarium care. It is important to note that maintaining some sort of schedule is recommended; that way, you do not forget to clean the aquarium. Some might ask, "But aquariums have filters, why do I need to do anything? After all, no one filters the water for the fish in the lakes and rivers, and they do just fine". Consider this; the process of filtration in nature happens automatically. When it rains, freshwater is added to the water ecosystem. Currents and waves circulate large bodies of water like rivers and lakes. The vast volume of water dilutes most of the harmful toxins, aided by the plants which produce more oxygen while absorbing carbon dioxide from the air.

A fish tank's filter system can only do so much. Unlike self-cleaning nature, the tank remains as dirty as it is until you manually decide to clean it. Also, consider the fact that the water in an aquarium is microscopic compared to that of oceans or lakes. No one wants to replace an aquarium every few years because they were too lazy to clean it out. Filters most definitely hold the fort down to some extent, but when not properly maintained, they become clogged with fish waste, uneaten food decay and other potentially harmful products. If these clogs are not manually removed, the aquarium will become less and less habitable to fish.

1. Change the water

Poor water conditions are the cause of most illnesses in fish. Changing the water is arguably the most crucial part of routine aquarium maintenance. Here's how to get started. Remove a third of the water from the tank every week and replace it with fresh clean water. This will dilute most of the toxins present, and create a healthy environment for your fish. Do not allow waste build-up to be the reason why you meet your fish belly side up in the morning. For maximum efficiency, use water changers and siphons. They not only remove the water but also enable you to vacuum the debris accumulated at the bottom. Siphoning your fish tank is a simple process that only takes a few minutes. An aquarium vacuum kit can be found at most pet stores. When cleaning using a siphon, you have two options. Either the "submersion method" or the "suck-start method."

How to start a siphon using the submersion method

a.) Position your bucket at the bottom of the tank.

b.) Place the larger end of the tube inside the aquarium a few inches above the gravel. The other end of the tube should be pointed towards the bucket. If you have it, rest the open end of the gravel vacuum on top of the aquarium gravel.

c.) Place the larger tube opening on the fish tank and let the air inside so it gets displaced by water. The remaining length of tubing should be lowered inside the tank, slowly leaving very little air inside the tube.

d.) Grab the narrow end of the tube and seal the opening using your finger. Be careful not to break the seal.

e.) Lift the opening of the discharge and lower it into the bucket. When you have ensured that the vacuum end is still at the bottom of the tank, remove your finger from the discharge end to allow water to begin to flow.

f.) Move the vacuum end of the tube around the tank while making sure the other end remains inside the bucket. If you have an extra pair of hands to help you out, the process may be much easier, but a single person can still do this.

How to start a siphon using the suck-start method

a.) It is important to have a giant-sized bucket with the capacity to hold a lot of water. Place your bucket under the aquarium.

b.) Grab the vacuum kit. Most vacuum kits have a plastic tube that ranges from two to eighteen inches (5.1 cm to 47.5 cm) Such a tube has its other end open by half an inch. Gauge the size of your tank and ensure that the kit you purchase can reach the furthest point inside the tank, go over it and also reach inside the bucket.

c.) The siphon procedure is the easiest because it does two things at the same time, which is; remove the solid waste from the fish tank and also change about 25% of the water. It is a less complicated but still an inexpensive method of maintaining a fish tank with minimal effort because once you have your rigid tube connected to the half-inch tube, your work is done. The kit will do its job.

How to start a siphon with your mouth

If you find yourself in a position where you are not able to acquire all the necessary kits to help you with the siphoning process, the last course of action should then be; starting a siphon with your mouth.

a.) Just as before, ensure you have placed the bucket under the fish tank.

b.) Place the larger opening of the tube at the bottom of the aquarium, and position the vacuum end a few inches above the gravel. If you own a gravel vacuum, you can place the end of the tube directly on the gravel.

c.) Initiate suction by placing your mouth on the discharge opening. Suck lightly at the end of the tube to get the water flowing. Make sure that the end of the tube is lower than the container from which you are siphoning water.

d.) Water should immediately begin to flow, then quickly remove the piece from your mouth and place the opening inside the bucket. As the water flows, move the other end of the tube around the tank to suck up any debris.

e.) When you have removed enough water, place your thumb on the opening of the tube and face the tube upwards to rise above the tank level. Once this is done, the process will come to a halt. If you would like to siphon more water, you will need to repeat the process over again.

When you are using a siphon connected to the sink, turning the sink knobs up higher is the only way to speed up the process. Be sure to thoroughly wash your hands before and after inserting your hands inside the tank. This is because aquatic life reacts very negatively to dirt, bacteria and even soap, so wash your hands with warm water to kill off anything that might negatively affect your skin or your fish.

2. Refill the tank with warm, dechlorinated water

Before adding in any water, measure it with a thermometer to make sure it is at the same level as the water in the tank. Then, using a bucket, add it to the tank. Follow up with water treatment from a bottle conditioner, which one can find at a pet store. Read the manufacturer's instructions for the recommended amount to mix into the water.

Always use separate items for aquarium supplies and equipment and never mix the materials with other household items. This is to avoid the germs and soap that are present on the surfaces of the rest of the containers that come in contact with the fish's environment. For example, instead of using a fork to mix the conditioner inside the water, use an aquarium net.

3. Test and monitor the water parameters

If you plan on having an aquarium, then a water testing kit should be included in your maintenance budget. However, before you buy one, you can check to see if;

- Your fish shop offers free water testing.
- The fish shop offers a maintenance service like testing the water (periodically) once a month.
- Most fish shops or pet stores have a flat rate for monthly testing that they can quote you.

Ultimately, the method with the least amount of hassle should work well for you. Ammonia and nitrate rapidly increase in a tank, so to avoid fish loss, testing the water can prove to be a critically important step. Keep a log of the test results so that you can observe the pattern of environmental changes in the tank and adjust accordingly. Keep in mind that an aquarium does not need to be cleaned every single day. Doing this disrupts the beneficial bacteria's procedures and might alter the levels of nitrogen in the water, thereby causing a spike in ammonia and nitrites. Colony rich areas, such as the filter and the substrate, should be cleaned every few weeks.

Nitrites

Elevation of nitrate levels is always an indicator of trouble. During the startup of a new fish tank, nitrate levels sometimes increase so much that they can even kill the fish, something we are trying to avoid. These tests should be carried out monthly or if a fish becomes sick or dies.

You can add one to three tablespoons of salt per gallon of water to reduce the effects of nitrite toxicity. Water changes have proven to be the easiest way to reduce elevated nitrate levels. Nitrites should be undetectable at all times (except during cycling). New aquariums should have ammonia and nitrite levels checked regularly to avoid the "Fresh Tank Syndrome" problem. If nitrite is detectable, be sure to test for ammonia as well.

Nitrates
Levels of nitrates should be maintained below ten ppm in freshwater, and five ppm or lower in saltwater and reef aquariums. Nitrate is a source of algae problems, and though not as toxic as ammonia or nitrite, it should still be monitored, particularly when one is in the process of breeding new fish. Young fish are usually more sensitive to nitrate that older fish, so monthly tests, water changes and maintenance of low nitrate levels give way to a healthy functioning aquatic life system.

pH
The most frequent cause of fish stress is acid-base balance in the water. Sudden changes in pH levels are not tolerable to fish. Even changes of as little as 0.2 could lead to death, yet pH remains one of the most overlooked factors. pH must remain stable. pH in the range of 6.5 – 7.5 is suitable for most species. Gradual changes in pH are less extreme in the short term but can eventually be just as harmful to fish health as a sudden shift in pH.

To acclimate your new fish, find out the pH of the fish shop you bought it at. Also, keep in mind that if you plan on using tap water, you will need to let it sit overnight because gasses will have dissolved inside the water because of the constant pressure it has been under. Then, after you have let it sit, you can then test the water.

Things that contribute to changes in pH include:

- Fish and plant waste present
- Water evaporation
- Topping off the water
- Water hardness

Buffering capability also affects Ph. The biological filter uses the carbonate in the water as aquariums mature, and the aquarium may lose its buffering ability, contributing to drastic pH changes. Consult with your local fish store for buffering compounds to increase the water alkalinity to stabilize the pH level. Aim for a monthly pH test or if you notice your fish gets sick or dies.

KH (carbonate hardness)
KH is a measure of pH stability. If it drops close to 4.5 dH (degree hardness) or 80 ppm, you should make sure to keep a keen eye on it. If hardness drops below 45 dH, the pH of the aquarium water will crash. A half teaspoon of baking soda will raise the kH by approximately one DH (17.8 ppm) for every twenty-five gallons of water.

Ammonia
Swift measures should be taken in addressing toxic levels of ammonia that may be present in the tank. Ammonia can be present in a non-ionized form (NH_3), or the ionized form (NH_4+) known as ammonium. The amount of toxic ammonia (NH_3) must ideally be at zero, but the non-toxic

ionized form (NH4 +) of ammonium in aquarium water is often present.

Ammonia may be raised by:

- A start-up cycle in a new tank
- Dirty water due to neglect
- Clogged and dirty filters
- Overstocked tank caused by excess food
- Use of medication that disrupts the biological cycle

Testing should be done at least once a month or when a fish becomes sick or dies.

Phosphate

If you have high growth in algae, test for phosphates. A leading cause of increased phosphate is dry fish food, which comes in the form of overfeeding the fish with low quality food. Often, low-quality fish food typically contains high levels of phosphate, which then leads to all those worrisome algae problems. Filtering products that eliminate phosphate from the water are available, and they can be added to your filter media.

The water parameters that need to be tested include ammonia, nitrite, nitrate, pH, hardness, alkalinity and possibly phosphate. Water temperature is also essential. It is important to remember this; not all fish like lukewarm water. Fish that live inside aquariums fall into two categories, which are cool water and tropical water fish. Cool water fish, for example, Goldfish, Koi and White Cloud Mountain Minnow, prefer cool water. Tropical fish like Tetras, Red Swordtails, Dwarf Gouramis, Guppies and Bettas need to be housed in a heated tank with a temperature range of 75-80°F (24-27°C). Because of the drastic differences in temperature, cool water and tropical water fish should not be housed together in the same tank.

4. Cycle the tank before adding fish

"Cycling a tank" means to take the steps necessary to bring the water conditions up to where they are healthy for the fish. What this means is that before any fish is introduced, water needs to be monitored, and the environment needs to 'grow' beforehand. Technically, you should purchase the fish one week after you have purchased the tank to allow for the healthy micro-organisms in the tank to grow. These micro organisms break down waste and help keep water safe for fish. The one-week timeline for letting the water run prior to fish introduction is recommended by most fish experts. Starting an aquarium the right way is just as important as taking care of it.

Most new aquarium kits come with a small box that you can use to add the required elements for cycling, or you can buy it at a pet store separately. Adding a little fish food can also cycle the tank because the food will begin to break down, thereby initiating the cycling process. A word of caution: never attempt to cycle your tank when your fish are inside. Until the water parameters are safe for the fish, exposing them to altered levels of an acid-base could cause illness to the fish or, worse still, kill them.

5. Do not overfeed fish

Starving a fish is quite a difficult thing to do. All they require is one feeding a day or two at most. Some people even skip a day or two of feeding to give the fish enough time to clear their digestive systems. Most of them require three to five fish pellets a day or a similar amount of flakes. However, keep in mind that bigger, more sedentary fish may go longer than smaller, more active fish between meals. Ensure you have different food for the different types of fish in your tank since fish do not all eat the same thing. If you have a lot of bottom feeders, including more sinking pellets, it's a good idea rather than just relying on flake foods. Include algae wafers if you have algae eating fish when introducing the food in the tank. Excess food is unhealthy to fish because it can:

- Lead to disease
- Cause a spike in the aforementioned chemicals
- Lead to a dirty tank
- Create unfavorable conditions like excess algae growth
- Lead to a snail outbreak

Many fishkeepers place their fish on a feed / fast schedule and use one or two days a week to skip feeding the fish, thereby keeping the tank cleaner and fish much healthier. In simple terms, feed your fish at the same time every day and remember that goes into a fish, must come out, so the more you feed your fish, the dirtier the tank will get.

6. Manage the light in and around your aquarium

Why do you need lights in an aquarium? Well, the algae (plants that grow inside) need this light to survive. Managing algae can sometimes prove to be complicated. So how can one enjoy the sight of their aquarium without running the risk of overgrowing algae? One way is to decide where you want to place your tank, preferably somewhere with no access to direct sunlight. When given the chance of sunlight exposure, algae will grow to the point where your tank will look like a bush drowning in water. You can use an algae magnet to help you easily vacuum up the algae. Another way to deal with algae is by keeping a snail or algae eating fish in the tank, but do your research to find out which aquatic species work well together in an aquarium, and which don't. You also want to keep the tank away from drafty basements, furnaces, and fireplaces. Find a spot where the temperature and sunlight stay level throughout the day.

Remember; the light present in the fish tank is purely for your human eyes to enjoy. The light during the day is pretty much exactly what the fish need, and at night, there is no real need for light. Twelve hours of daylight is enough, and if there is no one home, there is no need for you to leave the lights on. Also, you could turn it off at night when you are sleeping or when you go to work in the morning.

However, if you have live plants, they will need twelve hours of direct overhead lighting a day which means placement of the tank in a sunlit area. Live plants can help in keeping algae levels in check because they tend to suck up most of the nutrients required by the algae in order to survive. If you are ever unsure about anything, call your local pet store to inquire.

7. Do your research before purchasing

Have you ever heard of the rule "one inch of fish per gallon"? Well, here is something you might want to consider before adhering to that rule; fish start small, but as time passes by, they continue to grow to different sizes and eventually, if you have fifty fish inside your aquarium, it might be time to upgrade to a larger fish tank. When buying fish, consider the purchase based on the projection of how big they might grow and what your tank will look like once they are mature.

Also, don't just buy fish with the most beautiful fins or buy solely out of looks. Instead, consult and research on which type of fish work well together. I will cover this topic in the next chapter. Beware of the kind of fish that are hostile to one another. An example is the Neon Tetra, which is more susceptible to aggression from other more aggressive fish like Cichlids or Barbs, but lives well with Guppies, Mollies, Loaches, Cardinal Tetras, Corydoras, and Catfish, all of which is a diverse and beautiful set of fish to admire.

Knowing what fish you are purchasing and what their needs are, helps you to understand how many fish can safely live in your tank. Always add the most aggressive fish last so other, less aggressive, but still ornery fish can settle into their spots. When you intend to breed your fish, make sure your tank contains extra volume to house the offspring! Attendants at pet stores should be equipped with this information, but, unfortunately, very few of them are. Understand the potential magnitude of fish, their behavior, their space requirements and with which fish can get along.

8. Clean the filter

Open up your filter to access its internal components so you can clean it thoroughly. The recommended frequency is once a month. If your filter gets too dirty, the best option is usually to replace it. Take some water from the tank and pour it inside a bowl. Take apart the filter parts and swirl them around inside the bowl. If the filter chamber shows signs of algae growth, gently scrub it with an algae brush using water from the tank. If the stains refuse to come out, replace the filter. An excellent way to ascertain whether your filters are clogged is to pay attention to the pace of water cycles in the tank. If water flow is slow, it means it's either time to scrub the filters or replace them altogether.

Frequency of maintenance

First of all, here is a list of equipment you will need:

- Water bucket
- Siphon
- Algae scrubber
- Filter brush
- Aquarium safe glass cleaner
- Cleaning cloths/paper towels
- Replacement filter media
- Scissors to trim plants
- Plant fertilizer

The aquarium bucket should only be used for that purpose. You can even have two separate buckets that you can use to change the water though it is not necessary. You can store these items inside the bucket for a more convenient time when needed again.

Daily

- Monitor your fish's' behavior when they are feeding to see if anything might be off.
- Do a visual scan of the filter and lights and any other equipment you may have set up.
- Check on your fish to make sure they look healthy.
- If, after ten to fifteen minutes, uneaten food remains in the tank, take note of this so that you can reduce the frequency of feeding.
- Ensure the temperature is correct for the fish you have in the tank.
- Record your daily observations in a log or an aquarium journal. It is not necessary to record everything, but it is essential to record anything that seems out of the ordinary. The temperature dropping by a degree, for example, is not a big deal, but if it falls by a degree four days in a row, it's an indication that something is not working properly with your heater.

Weekly

- Clean the aquarium walls using a non-ammonia aquarium safe cleanser, or simply use a damp cloth.
- Count the fish. Smaller species can decompose quickly in the event of fish death, resulting in spikes of ammonia and nitrite, and eventually high levels of nitrate.
- To be able to dislodge any debris that may be stuck, gently shake the plants, whether they are live plants or not.

- Scrape inside the glass to remove algae, and then give it a few minutes to settle down before siphoning them out.
- Use filter floss to catch microscopic bubbles that are responsible for cloudy water.
- Siphon substrate to remove debris.
- Partially change the water as the last step after all the other tasks have been completed. Use water that is treated, and if possible, aged.
- Maintain a maintenance log of the actions you have taken and record anything unusual you may have seen.

Monthly
- Replace filter inserts, cartridges, floss, carbon, and Algone. Rinse the entire filter if needed. However, avoid replacing all the filter media at the same time. Instead, retain part of the media to avoid losing too large a portion of the beneficial biological colonies. You can replace the remaining part the following month. Mechanical filter media like foam can be replaced once or twice a year.
- Replace exhaustible media such as activated carbon or zeolite.
- For proper operation, inspect tubing, ties, airstones, skimmers and other parts.
- Test your water parameters: pH, ammonia, nitrite, and nitrate. This should be the very first thing you do before any other checks that you do.
- Check the expiration dates printed on the boxes and bottles of the aquarium supplies you use. Expired kits give false readings which may, in turn,

prompt someone to take action where they should not be.

Periodic
- Fertilize live plants
- Replace light bulbs once a year, regardless of whether they have burned out or not.

Each aquarium is different and will need a maintenance plan that best fits its specific conditions. Make sure to avoid an overstocked and overfed aquarium as it is far more challenging to maintain.

3 TYPES OF FISH SPECIES YOU CAN HAVE IN YOUR FISH TANK

The first thing to do is to find out whether your water is fresh or salty. Therefore, you will know what fish species to put in it. Optimally, you want something sturdy, affordable and colorful with an interesting personality. However, here are a few key factors to consider before deciding what fish goes into your tank:

Volume and tank layout

Every fish species requires specific living conditions. From the type of space such as sand, rocky, more plant-based or isolated caves to fish that prefer to live together in large groups, it is important to find out the specific needs of each type of fish you intend to mix.

Water quality parameters

Some fish species like hard water with a high pH, whereas others prefer soft water with a much lower ph. Do not try to balance out the pH levels somewhere in the middle because you mixed fish with different water parameter requirements.

Aggressive nature

Aggressive nature is species specific. Some fish like the Angelfish can be quite aggressive. Always add these fish as the last ones, to allow the other less aggressive types to settle into their spots first. Consider community-minded fish that are friendly and can get along with others in the same environment.

Fish diet

Choose fish that feed on more of the same kind of food; that way, they all get something to eat. Otherwise, the more aggressive type of fish might consume all the dinner, and the little ones might go hungry without you knowing it. Spread out your meals to limit competition because while some fish feed at the surface or through the water columns, others like Loaches sift through the substrate.

Best Freshwater Community Aquarium Fish

1. Neon Tetra

They are not only vibrant looking fish but also require very little space to live. They are also friendly and not picky eaters. Neon Tetra are considered the most popular fish amongst fish keepers and the most beginner-friendly fish. They're roughly about an inch (2.2cm) in length and like to be kept in a school of three to six. They are omnivores and eat worms, shrimp, brine, insects and plants and can live for up to ten years. Because of their peaceful temperament, they live well with other fish. Keep in mind that they tend to be easy prey for the more aggressive type of fish like Angelfish.

2. Guppies

Guppies are adaptable to a wide variety of water conditions, hence their popularity. They are also quite colorful, ranging in a variety of colors from orange to blue, and are easy to take care of. As livebearers, they reproduce very quickly, so if you don't want to have more fish than you already do at the moment, the best thing to do would be to separate the males from the females. Their average lifespan is about two years but they can live up to three years in proper tank conditions. These easy-going fish reside in water with temperatures in a range of 50F – 84F (10-29C) and will eat flakes, pellets and even their own offspring.

3. Oscars

Oscars are thought to be one of the most intelligent fish species, so much so that they can be trained to do tricks and can recognize strangers. This large-sized fish, about 13 inches (33cm) in length, requires a tank of at least 30 gallons for better living conditions. Temperatures between 74°C to 81°C help to strengthen their immune system and preventing disease. Oscars thrive best when kept in pairs, or a group of five or more from when they are young. Keep in mind they can grow very big, very fast. They tend to produce a lot more waste and are carnivorous in nature, and because of this, they require a bit more maintenance. Although an Oscar fish can be aggressive, they will share the tank with other fish, but keep in mind; the smaller tank fish might look like a good meal at any moment. They have a lifespan of about ten years and prefer a tank with rock ledges.

4. Zebra Danio

Zebra Danios are prolific breeders and can easily be recognized by their stripped zebra-patterned body. With a five-year lifespan, they can endure an impressive range of water conditions and can grow anywhere between 1-3 inches (5-7cm). They are also one of the few fish species that mate for life. This peaceful fish grows to about two inches in size and can get along with other fish like Barbs, Corydoras Catfish, and Swordtails. They do best when they are kept in a group of five or more, with water temperatures in the range of 64 to 75F. These active fish enjoy eating small, live or frozen invertebrates like worms and fresh vegetable matter. Danios are also known to jump, so you may want to keep your tank covered! Other Danio breeds to consider include Leopard, and Pearl Danios.

5. Goldfish

The prized aquatic pet; the Goldfish! Not only is it a pocket friendly purchase, but it also requires little care. It's beautiful to look at and is also friendly especially during feeding time. These tiny fish interact with their owners and can be trained to accept food from the hand. The standard Goldfish (*Carassius Auratus*) is particularly suitable for beginners because they are exceptionally tough and need less devoted attention than some other breeds. They grow to about 12 to 14 inches, so they require 30 gallons of water per fish.

Their diet consists of spirulina algae, vegetables, and food higher in carbohydrate content than protein content. Although they are not aggressive in nature, if they happen to come across a smaller fish that fits in their mouth, they will definitely eat it. For this fish to live well, they require quite an ample space, so no, don't buy a bowl for your goldfish. Goldfish are just fine being by themselves and don't suffer from lack of company. They can live well enough with the Zebrafish and the ornamental Minnows. They can also be fed every two weeks. That's why they make great pets for travelers. Goldfish can live between five to ten years, making them a good fish companion.

Other fish species to keep include:

- **Barbs:** Cherry, Gold, Odessa, Rosy, and Tico Barbs are good choices. Tinfoil and Spanner Barbs are to be avoided due to their colossal size. Tiger Barbs tend to nip and be quarrelsome, so you might want to avoid those. Some species are considered semi-aggressive, so buy six or more to reduce fin nipping.

- **Rasboras:** Harlequins, Lambchop and Scissortails are good choices. They are peaceful, grow to about two inches long and are also readily available at local pet stores. For a striking display of colors, get a group of six or more.

- **Catfish (some varieties):** Bronze or Gold Corys, Spotted Cory, Bandit Cory, and Panda Cory, are excellent. Although they do live for twenty years plus, you may want to avoid Plecos unless you have a large tank or have a local pet shop that will take them back when they grow too big. Also, they jump so keep your tank lid covered.

- **Rainbowfish:** Boesmans, Neon, and Celebes are all good. They can grow up to six inches long and generate some pretty vibrant colors as they enter into adulthood. Keep the temperature at 74-78 degrees Fahrenheit and have at least 30 gallons of water. They play well with Rasboras, Catfish Danios, and other non-aggressive Cichlids. Feed them Color Flakes, Spirulina Flakes, and Betta Treats in the amount they can consume in two minutes.

- **White Cloud Mountain Minnows:** This tiny fish is only about 1 inch (2-3cm) in size and not demanding. These brightly colored fish can live for three years and preferably, in a school of six or more. These micro predators feed on worms, small insects, crustaceans and other varieties of zooplankton.

Beautiful as they may be, some fish like Convict Cichlids can prove to be too aggressive for community tanks. The best option is always to have these fish separate from the rest in a different tank.

Here are some angry fish you can avoid:

- **Convict cichlids** – they are a territorial bunch that have been known to pick fights with other larger species of fish. These convicts become even more aggressive during the mating season.

- **Tiger Barbs** – A single tiger barb will terrorize smaller fish and can end up killing it if they are not kept in schools. They will mostly fight among themselves if they are kept in schools. Either pair them up with larger fish or with no fish at all.

- **Snakeheads -** they are called so because of the flat scaled covered head they possess. They are very violent towards smaller fishes and will attack and consume any fish that is smaller than them. They are carnivores; hence, a live diet is right for them, but they can also feed on small chunks of meat too. A key thing to consider is that they are also expensive.

- **Freshwater Stingrays** – as long as they are not provoked, they will not attack. However, once they do attack, they can be quite dangerous and cause immense pain. There are numerous stingray varieties, each with its own set of rules. You can add them in a separate tank together with Cichlids and some species of Severums to spruce things up a bit.

- **Angelfish** – Angelfish become aggressive when feeding time approaches. They get along fine when they are much younger, but as they get larger, most Angelfish groups will start to have a dominant abuser. Even if that abuser fish is removed, another will take its place. They are rarely territorial, but it is advisable to make sure that there is more than enough room for all the Angelfish you wish to keep.

- **Gouramis** – They feel a need to establish some sort of hierarchy in the tank and will become aggressive towards fish that threaten their established territory. All varieties of Gouramis are incredibly territorial, especially towards small fish.

- **Plecostomus** – Plecos are only aggressive to other Plecos but take fish cannibalism to a whole new level. They will feed on other fish and even consume the dead ones too. Get some Omega One Algae discs and keep your Plecos on a very healthy diet to avoid such behavior. They are nocturnal, and they can sometimes live for up to 15 years and can live in water temperatures of 72-76 degrees Fahrenheit.

Other aggressive fish include Rainbow Shark, Betta fish, Red-Bellied Piranhas, Leopard Bush Fish, Bucktooth Tetra and Green Spotted Puffer.

If you are new to fish keeping, the best thing to do would be to start slow with just a few fish. Observe them and learn how to take care of different types of fish and also get accustomed to routine tank maintenance. Once you have done this for a couple of months, or even a year, you can then expand your school of fish or buy another tank altogether.

Best Saltwater Aquarium Fish

Usually, the most significant consideration for a mixed-species tank is size. Having more water adds extra cushioning for lapses in maintenance. In short, the bigger the aquarium and the more water capacity it has, the better for the fish.

1. Pajama Cardinalfish

This is one of the most unique choices in saltwater fish keeping. The pajama cardinalfish has a yellow/green face and front with a black band around its middle and a bright polka dot tail. They are shy fish that prefer to come out at night and can be kept in a twenty-gallon tank. If you are planning to have a school of these, you'll need about thirty gallons. Ensure you have a lot of live plants and rocks for these shy fish to feel right at home.

2. Banggai or Kaudern's Cardinalfish

This attractive carnivore boasts of bold, black stripes along its shimmering silver body highlighted in small white spots. These easy going fish are slow simmers which should be housed in a thirty-gallon tank. Scape the aquarium with a generous amount of live rock, caves, crevices and enough swimming space. Feeding should be done several times a day with limited portions of a well-balanced diet, which includes enriched frozen brine shrimp and Mysis shrimp, along with a quality marine pellet or flake food.

3. Neon Blue Goby

The electric blue coloration of the neon goby makes this fish a prized addition in your tank. They are not picky when it comes to food and will even help you out with your algae problems because they actively scour surfaces for freshwater algae. It is critical to provide high aeration and strong water movement to ensure the health of the Neon Blue Goby, which can be achieved by using powerheads. A twenty gallon tank will do just fine for this intriguing fish full of personality.

4. Clownfish

Clownfish are particularly easy to care for, especially the False Percula variety. They mostly feed on dry pellets and frozen food. Captive bred species vary in that their markings are sometimes different from their wild caught counterparts. Captive bred clowns can be maintained together in the aquarium, with the female being larger than its male counterpart. Captive bred Percula Clowns are initially orange and white but later mature to develop dark black lines between their white stripes. When Clownfish are born, they are all males, and the largest fish in a group has the ability to change itself into a female, mostly during mating.

5. Firefish

Also known as the Firefish Goby, Fire Goby, and Magnificent or Fire Dartfish, they are long, thin fish with a white or light-colored body and a bright red, orange, and/or magenta posterior. They are sweet tempered fish with lots of personality that also require rocky crags or outcroppings where they can hide when stressed. A 20-gallon or more extensive system with moderate lighting conditions and a moderate current passing over the live rock "reef" is preferred. Their diet should be high in vitamin enriched brine fish (live or frozen), Mysis shrimp, and prepared marine foods.

6. Damselfish

Damselfish are rarely aggressive, as long as they have enough hiding spaces like rocks and caves. They range in colors from deep blues, orange and even black and white stripes. They are also intriguing species of Damselfish; for example, the Blue Sapphire Damselfish turns completely black when stressed out, which also helps them avoid predators. Provide plenty of live rock with multiple hiding places to break up territories and decrease aggression. There are a number of Damselfish varieties, so have a consultation with your local pet store to find out the exact breed and its exact needs.

Other types of saltwater fish perfect for keeping include Tangs, Watchman Goby, Chalk Bass, Dottyback, Firefish, Coral Beauties, Talbot's Damsel, Wrasses, Blenny Fish, Butterfly Fish, Mollies, Green Chromis, Longnose Hawkfish, Royal Gramma Basslet, and Big Eye Black Bar Soldierfish.

Black Banded Cat Shark, Goldbar Wrasse and Clown Triggerfish can prove to be a bit difficult since they do not play well with others and also require lots of water.

Saltwater fish are indeed much more difficult to keep than freshwater. Keep in mind that it is not only messier but also more expensive to maintain a saltwater tank, and the fish tend to be more expensive as well. However, if you are up to the task and have a healthy budget, then this option might be good for you. Overall, there is no one right way to set up an aquarium. Do your research before buying anything in order to make sure all species will thrive in their new homes.

4 CHOOSING THE BEST FISH TANK SIZE FOR YOUR HOME OR BUSINESS

Novice aquarists often forget to consider fish tank size when acquiring one. Without paying attention to the size of your fish tank and the species you intend on housing, you could end up with stunted growth for your fish, aggressiveness because of territory fights and even unstable water parameters. All of these issues could lead to the death of your fish. A key consideration to make is whether or not the tank fits both the fish and your own habitat. This is because an aquarium tank that doesn't fit your home will hamper your ability to appreciate your fish. There are so many options to choose from, which often leaves a buyer more confused. However, there are a few key considerations you need to make that will ensure you make the best decision for your lifestyle and the lifestyle of your new friends.

The bigger the tank, the better

Why is this usually the case? An unavoidable circumstance is the amount of waste fish excrete, which include: poop, pee and uneaten food. These substances break down and end up becoming toxic to the water. This is one of the main reasons why we do water changes. The smaller your tank is, the more these chemicals will build up.

Picture what happens when you add one tablespoon of coffee to your cup of water; it goes immediately dark, right? Now, picture adding this same tablespoon of coffee to a swimming pool. The coffee will dissolve to the point where you will not be able to spot at which point it originated from. This same concept applies to your aquarium. The smaller it is, the more buildup of toxic chemicals there will be, which will force you to perform regular water changes. A large tank leaves lots of room for error, which as a beginner, you definitely might make.

However, if you are on a tight budget, it is best to think about this in reverse order. Instead of first buying an aquarium then pondering over what type of fish you should keep in it, first, decide the budget for your fish, project the growth of the fish in terms of size, note their traits in terms of where they prefer to live, i.e., big caves, schools, reefs etc. then, buy the aquarium.

With these considerations in mind, you will be able to see just how big of an aquarium you might need. Big aquariums make fish happy because they have a lot of room to swim around in. It's not only easier to maintain a large tank, especially if you invest in the vacuum kits, it also makes fish less stressed and less aggressive. It takes longer for ammonia to spike in larger tanks, so you have more time to react if something goes wrong. It is far easier to stabilize a 100-gallon tank than it is a 30-gallon tank just like it is easier to stabilize a 30-gallon tank than a ten-gallon tank. Water conditions in larger tanks are more likely to be within healthy tolerance as opposed to the alternative.

Avoid the starter tank

Save up enough money to buy exactly what you think you will buy in the future. Why? Because more often than not, aquarists tend to think of beginning their journey with a 'starter tank' with the hope of buying a bigger tank later on, but never actually do. There is no harm in purchasing a 30-gallon tank so long as you know that the fish you intend to keep will not grow up to a size that will require more space than that of a 30-gallon tank. For example, you might want to purchase an Oscar but, with a 30-gallon tank, your Oscar will not only feel cramped, but it will also become increasingly hostile towards the rest of the fish because the minimum tank requirements for an Oscar is a 60-gallon tank. Also, cramped spaces reduce the lifespan of fish, so if you want your fish to live longer, give it the space it needs. However, you can comfortably house Neon Tetras in a 30-gallon tank. It's all in the species of fish you decide to keep and their space requirements.

How deep are your pockets?

It is pretty clear that the larger the aquarium, the more expensive it will be. For example, a twenty gallon glass aquarium can range anywhere between $100 to $200, depending on the type and where you buy it, whereas, a fifty gallon tank will cost you anywhere from $600 to $1800 or more, depending on your purchase location, brand, and type preference. All Glass and Oceanic are decent brand names, but Top Fin is merely All Glass with a generic logo, and most tanks are not branded at all, so don't overthink about branding. Instead, when choosing an aquarium, think about the space your fish will need and the space available at your home where you intend to keep the fish. Let these two things be part of the determining factors for the eventual size you pick out.

41

When picking out a tank, it is paramount that you check the seal. Check all the sealant for cracks or missing pieces inside and out, especially the seal down by the trim. Resealing a tank takes a lot of hours scraping with a razor blade. You want to avoid this at all cost, especially if your purchase is brand new. Deeper chips and cracks especially on the corners are red flags. It is better to see the tank filled with water; that way you can personally ensure that there is no leakage of any kind before purchase.

Do some math

Consider this; a gallon of freshwater at 70 degrees Fahrenheit weighs 8.329 pounds. When you consider the water, the weight of the tank itself, the gravel and decorations, and everything else that will go inside it, a full ten-gallon tank will weigh somewhere around 100 pounds. A full 55-gallon tank will weigh around 550-600 pounds, depending on what you have in it. For any tank ten gallons or larger, a dedicated aquarium stand is not only beneficial but also necessary. You can get away with placing the tank on another surface but be sure that it will be able to hold the weight down once you have everything in place. You don't want to start breaking furniture in your house, or worse still, the foundation. You'd rather have it in the basement if it is too big than in other areas of the house.

At the end of the day, there is no one size fits all when it comes to choosing an aquarium.
However, the general rule of thumb to be adhered to are:

- The larger the tank, the happier the fish.
- Bigger tanks are easier to maintain.

- Choose your aquarium based on the type of fish you intend to keep.
- Don't just choose the right size. If you can find and afford a bigger one, go for it.

Surface area consideration

The surface area is barely taken into account with the 'gallon per inch' rule of thumb. Respiration in fish is achieved by eliminating dissolved oxygen from the water, and then expiring carbon dioxide back into the tank water. The water's ability to hold oxygen and carbon dioxide is crucial; thus, the surface area is of fundamental importance and cannot be underestimated. Think of it this way; a lake supports more fish than a pond.

Oxygen and CO2

While you can find almost any shape aquarium at your local pet store, consider the surface area available for your fish to live comfortably. Since the surface is where oxygen enters the aquarium and where carbon dioxide is emitted from, the value of the surface area cannot be overlooked. The capacity for the exchange of oxygen and carbon dioxide depends mainly on the surface area the aquarium can handle, which in turn reflects on the quality of life of the fish.

Warm or cold water

Tropical fish and cold water fish are both distinct, and these distinctions must be considered when selecting the right sized aquarium. Facilitate between 20 and 25 square inches of surface area per inch of adult tropical fish and between 25 and 30 square inches of surface area per inch of cold water fish, as they usually have high body mass and need more oxygen.

5 TYPES OF FISHTANKS

Freshwater Tropical Aquarium

Novice aquarists should feel very comfortable starting with this tank. The water temperature typically ranges from 72 to 84 Degrees Fahrenheit. They are easy for beginners, and quite common too because they do not require fancy chemical additives (except the necessary chemicals like chlorine removers) or expensive light fixtures. They are also more affordable compared to most other aquariums. The Freshwater Tropical aquarium provides a wide variety of fish to choose from. Although there are species of freshwater aquarium fish that are rather expensive, the majority of freshwater fish are really affordable. They are an excellent place for every aquarist to start.

Even though managing a freshwater aquarium is not too difficult, it does require some effort if you do want to create a suitable environment for your fish to be happy. For example, simple measures such as managing the water's pH levels are vital to the health and sustainability of the environment your fish need to live and thrive. Depending on the species, most freshwater fish require a pH level between 6.6 and 7.8. Some basic criteria for keeping your tropical freshwater aquarium are daily water changes, water treatment and tank cleanings, all of which are easier to do once you start getting the hang of it. These aquariums can be your dining room's centerpiece, the perfect balance for your study, or the ideal backdrop for your living room.

Coldwater Aquariums

One of the most common coldwater species kept in a coldwater aquariums is the Goldfish. The typical temperature for such aquariums is 70 degrees or room temperature. Establishing a coldwater aquarium is as easy as installing the necessary equipment which could, in effect, significantly extend your fish's' lifespan. When you start shopping for species other than regular Goldfish, the coldwater freshwater fish may be a bit more costly. Good examples of domesticated coldwater fish habitats are the Koi and Goldfish ponds.

Marine Aquariums

Saltwater or Marine aquariums, as they are generally called, deliver a species of fish that freshwater tanks seemingly can't. Purchasing a tank like this will require salt to be mixed into the tank before adding any fish. They might require a little more effort to maintain so you can provide a sustainable fish ecosystem for saltwater fish. Marine fish are not only more sensitive to changes in water temperatures, but they are also more expensive than their freshwater counterparts.

For the sake of saving money, and more importantly, avoiding animal cruelty, it is advisable that a beginner starts with freshwater aquariums so that they can learn the ropes of what it means to care for fish, before taking on the mighty marine. The key to this hobby is patience. It is highly recommended that your journey begin with the freshwater aquariums, this way you can learn as you go and become proficient at fish keeping before moving on to other more advanced aquariums.

Don't get me wrong, I don't want to dissuade you. Marine aquariums are a worthwhile investment. They offer stunning views of the coral and quite unique invertebrates to give you a spectacular colorful masterpiece of a display or distraction in your home. There is so much automated equipment these days to help you get through this, but fishkeeping is no more an investment than any other hobby.

Brackish Aquariums

Brackish water is typically a mixture of saltwater and freshwater in a sense that it lies somewhere in-between and does not lean too far to either side. If you can picture the Mississippi River emptying into the Gulf of Mexico, that is brackish water. This is a type of aquarium that experts recommend experienced fish keepers own instead of beginners. The Pufferfish is a famous example of a brackish water fish, but most people don't have much success when keeping these types of fish because of the care required and the attention needed for water temperatures.

Breeder Tank

Breeder tanks are smaller and shallower than traditional tanks. This is because when the fish are spawning, they will need to be able to get to the water's surface quickly, and they can easily do this in shallower water. They have a protected filter to avoid injury of the fish. Limpid traps made of plastic can be inserted into the tank, which allow the fish to see each other while keeping them separated. These traps are useful because some fish become violent during or after breeding, so they act as a way of protecting the fish from instigating fights. When you have eggs and babies, these traps become useful because you can isolate the adults from the eggs and young, which will keep them from consuming the eggs.

There is a variety of tanks to choose from, but the most recommended is usually the freshwater fish tank because they:

- are easy to maintain
- are inexpensive
- offer a wide variety of fish
- provide a great fish tank for beginners

Acrylic Tank

These tanks have become popular due to advances in technology that have been made. Acrylic is stronger and weighs less than glass. It also provides some temperature insulation too. For those who live in colder climates, using acrylic tanks proves to be much more efficient and doesn't require a powerful heater, and will do a much better job at regulating the temperature.

One of the downsides is that it's much easier to get scratches on an acrylic tank, but then these scratches can be polished out. Another great benefit of acrylic tanks is that it can designed to almost any shape you want, so the options are more vast than those of glass. You won't have to deal with refraction when you buy an acrylic tank. As an option, if you want to have a fish tank overflow system installed, you can easily drill a hole in an acrylic tank to install that feature if you like.

Glass

Glass fish tanks are easy to find and rely on both a solid sealant and plastic frame to provide the fish tank with the protection and shape it needs. A common problem with glass tanks is because it's made of glass, and it's susceptible to breaking because it tends to be brittle. Most of the time, the issue with a glass fish tank is usually with the sealant, and that's why it is advised to carefully inspect the seals of your tank, and water test it before you buy it.

Glass tanks tend to stand up to scratches a whole lot better and are also cheaper than acrylic tanks. When it comes to the housing of a glass tank, you need to have a very strong frame or stand that can hold a glass tank because the same sized tank tends to weigh four to ten times more than acrylic tanks. Comparing a smaller tank, the price difference between the two is very noticeable as the size of the tank increases. Most glass tanks come in regular shapes like square or rectangular. Curved glass is rare, and it affects the appearance of the fish. This refraction is much more noticeable when the glass is thicker.

Interesting ways to display your fish:

- Coffee table aquariums
- Wall mounted aquariums
- Plater aquariums
- Alarm clock aquariums
- Double-sided tubed aquariums
- Bowfront aquariums

- Kits (If you are hoping to have a little more control over the equipment being used, you can choose a basic model that meets your size requirements.)

7 COMMON PROBLEMS WITH SMALL AQUARIUMS

Stunted growth

Here is a myth that should be debunked: *"Fish only grow to the size of the fish tank."*

The reason why this myth exists comes mainly from people that keep goldfish in a bowl. Goldfish are indeterminate growers, and, when placed in a tiny tank or bowl, they simply do not grow. This does not mean that they have reached their maximum size. It means that they are experiencing stunted growth, which is really bad for their health. To avoid permanently damaging the fish's health, it's advisable to get a larger tank.

Reduced lifespan

If stunted growth was not enough, the result is a reduced lifespan. There is scientific proof that suggests that:

- The stress caused by small spaces creates an excessive amount of tension around the fish's heart, thereby causing it to overwork.
- The stunted growth that results from keeping fish in small spaces causes organ failure because their internal organs lack space to grow, which could result in death.

Enhanced aggression

Behavioral implications like anxiety, stress and fear can be factors, making fish aggressive to other fish in the tank.

Popular Fish and Their Tank Size Requirements

Species	Minimum Recommend Tank Size (Individuals)	Minimum Recommend Tank Size (School)
Green Chromis	10 Gallons	40 Gallons
Common Clownfish	10 Gallons	60 Gallons
Royal Gramma	30 Gallons	100 Gallons
Oscar	60 Gallons	150 Gallons
Neon Tetra	5 Gallons	15 Gallons
Guppies	5 Gallons	20 Gallons

8 FISHKEEPING ON A BUDGET

Consider buying a used aquarium to keep your costs down

The price of a used, good quality, non-damaged aquarium is usually less than half of the store price, even when it's as good as new. If you plan on doing an onsite inspection of a used fish tank for sale by a seller, one of the first things you want to look at is all the seals in the corners of the fish tank. The second thing would be to inspect if the glass has any hairline cracks in it.

Adopt a fish instead

Because re-selling fish is almost impossible, most people who want to pass on their fish to someone else may simply give them away for free. There are Facebook pages for fish lovers, and other fish aficionado websites that give away their fish and adopt fish as well.

Turn down the temperature

Another major part of your aquarium energy bill is the heater that's required in almost every fish tank setup. Aquarium heaters use a lot of energy, which can lead to high electricity bills, so a great way to keep your costs down is to adjust to a lower temperature. This does not mean that you outright disregard the health conditions required for your fish to grow. Quite the contrary, it means choosing fish that do well in slightly lower temperatures (for example, 23°C/73.5°F instead of 26°C/79°F). Just a few degrees lower can save you lots of money, especially if the setup is large.

In general, tropical fish are most healthy in the range of 75-80°F (24-27°C). Cool water fish do better in temperatures between 60° and 75°F (15-24°C), but some of them enjoy water well below 70°F, which is not suitable for any tropical fish. The best temperature highly depends on the species of fish in the aquarium. After you have researched the fish you are interested in keeping, chose those that have similar temperature requirements within your budget.

Invest in high quality equipment

This might seem counterintuitive advice, but on the contrary, investing in high-quality fishkeeping equipment initially will save you a lot of money in the long run. This is especially true with equipment like filters and heaters, which can save you a whole lot of frustration too.

Some good filter brands include:

- Penn Plax Cascade Canister Aquarium Filter
- Fluval All-New 07 Series Performance Canister Filter
- Marineland Magniflow Canister
- EHEIM Classic External Canister Fish Tank Filter Media
- Penn Plax Cascade Canister Aquarium Filter Cascade

Opt for LED lights instead

LED lights are known for their energy saving quality. They can literally cut the electricity bill in half. If you have them in your living room, consider replacing the ones in your tank as well. Aquariums generally use quite a bit of power, so finding ways to save on the operation, care and maintenance cost of your fish tank is a smart thing for every aquarist to do.

Save money on plants
Everyone needs hardy, easy to care for plants. If you can find some that require no extra lights, specific water parameter and co2, then you won't have to worry about dying plants or CO_2 installations. Opt for plants that do not require too much extra product, for example, Java moss, Amazon sword, Java fern and Vallisneria. When you do this, you don't have to worry about sourcing fish food and plant food. You can find inexpensive plants in aquarium forums or groups where most people often give away plant trimmings for a low price. Some of them are usually willing to trade their plants for something else in return, which you might have to offer.

Replace as opposed to buy
Multiple reputable brands sell replacement parts for easily broken pieces of their filters, such as the impeller and the intake. You would much rather replace a single part than buy a whole new filter. This applies to not only the small parts but also the entire tank as well. If it starts to leak, most people assume it is broken and throw it out. Instead, leaking is usually a sign of a broken seal that can be re-sealed using aquarium silicone. The alternative is to buy a new tank, which is much more expensive.

9 THE BEST HOME LOCATION SET UP FOR YOUR AQUARIUM

Where you place your aquarium will depend on how big of an aquarium you want. Keep in mind that an aquarium cannot be placed 'anywhere.' Just because there is more than ample room in the garage does not mean the garage is the most suitable place to keep it.

Size matters

Size plays a significant role in the placement of your fish tank. The bigger it is, the heavier it will weigh, and the sturdier a surface you will need for installation. Here is a fact you might want to keep in mind: a gallon of water weighs almost nine pounds. That means that a five-gallon desk-top aquarium will weigh over 45 pounds!

Here are some examples of fish tank gallons by weight:

10 gallons (38 l) weight up to   110 lbs - (50 kilograms)

15 gallons (57 l) weight up to   175 lbs - (79 kilograms)

20 gallons (76 l) weight up to 230 lbs - (104 kilograms)

25 gallons (95 l) weight up to 295 lbs - (134 kilograms)

30 gallons (114 l) weight up to 360 lbs - (163 kilograms)

40 gallons (151 l) weight up to 465 lbs - (211 kilograms)

50 gallons (189 l) weight up to 650 lbs - (295 kilograms)

You need to find a space that can fit both your fish tank, and sturdy enough to able to carry its weight. Nano and desktop aquariums don't take up much room and can be perfect for office tables or kids rooms. If you place it on a table and the table breaks, that's an expensive accident, not to mention a big mess to clean up. Goodbye aquarium!

The best option when it comes to aquarium placement is a purpose-built fish tank table because it is built to support the weight of a fish tank. Also, most of them come with storage compartments for your equipment. Even with a specialty fish tank table, the floor of your home must also be strong enough to handle your aquarium weight, particularly if you have large aquariums. Make sure you pick a room that has level floors, otherwise choose a different location. Never level the aquarium by placing shims under the tank, this can put undue stress on the glass. A dresser can support a small aquarium, but the extra weight could make the dresser top heavy.

Fish tanks aren't exactly easy to move once they are set up, so proper planning is needed beforehand.

Place it within eye view

When it comes to taking care of fish, you want to place them somewhere where you can easily see and enjoy them. Unlike dogs or cats, these creatures are not able to follow you around the house. Aquariums are designed to be looked at. Also, having it in an easily accessible space can enable you to identify when something is amiss quickly. Be it an algae problem, a leaking tank, sick or dead fish, the sooner you can notice the problem the faster you can fix it. Place it where it will be seen, but not the busiest part of the house where there's a lot of traffic. The commotion alone can disturb the fish. Pick a place for your tank where you can see and appreciate it, but does not get in the way or be in danger of anyone crashing into it.

Electrical safety considerations

For the most part, an aquarium needs a minimum of three electrical sockets to take care of the filter, heater, and lighting. Your regular 15-amp household outlet with a high-quality power outlet will provide the electricity required for your aquarium with ease. However, to prevent electrocution, make sure the power strip is not placed on the floor and is away from potential water splashes. You should also make sure all the power cords are configured in a drip loop. This prevents water from running down the cord to the electrical outlet. This is the most critical safety precaution when choosing a location and setting up your fish tank.

A reef aquarium demands even more power. A power supply capable of handling one or more return pumps, wavemakers, protein skimmers, and reef lighting will be needed. If you construct an automated aquarium, you may need to install a wireless hub or controller to synchronize all the hardware. Dosing pumps and remote sensors will also need a power supply as well.

Keep electrical outlets free of salt crusts as saltwater creeps into them. Crusty outlets have the potential to start a fire. It is best to "map" the power requirements for more complex aquarium systems, and install a secure power strip setup without the risk of overloading the power supply.

Avoid areas subject to extreme hot or cold temperatures

Water temperature directly affects the biological processes of all aquatic life, including the fish, plants, snails and bacteria that help keep your tank healthy and clean. The best aquarium practice is to keep the tank where it will not be susceptible to extreme fluctuations in temperature because fish thrive in stable conditions much better. Rapid temperature changes occur throughout the day and can stress out your fish, which can lead to sickness or even death.

Be wary of nearby heating vents, fireplaces and space heaters, which can increase the temperature. You want to avoid sudden temperature fluctuations at all cost. Also, if you're going to set your aquarium up near a window, keep it closed. Though an aquarium heater can increase the water temperature, it cannot compensate for frigid temperatures.

Avoid sunlight

Direct sunlight hitting your tank encourages algae to grow. This does not mean you can't set up your aquarium near a window. Just remember to draw the curtains or place it near the window but away from direct contact with sunlight. Skylights should also be avoided. If you do not want to clean up thick green slime, then foregoing the very few benefits of light will save you a lot of trouble and headache later.

Consider the water source location

Your tank should be in a place where you can easily be able to access it because you will need to feed the fish, perform water changes, fix broken equipment, turn the aquarium lights on and off and perform the regular water parameter checks, filters, air pumps and heater controllers. It is ideal if you can place it in a space where you can be able to maneuver around the tank easily. This is especially important when you are performing water changes. The nearer you can position your aquarium to a source of freshwater, the less water you will have to carry back and forth.

Aquariums lose water through evaporation so weekly top-offs might be needed, and to reef aquariums, even daily due to water loss that happens as a result of protein skimming and evaporation. If distance is unavoidable, a simple cart or a hose directly connected to the water source will make it much easier to move a bucket of water. You can use a gravel vacuum to make life simpler, but keep in mind that some may only be able to reach up to about 50 feet.

Avoid high traffic areas
Aquarium tanks, whether glass or acrylic can easily be scratched, broken and cause leaks or get knocked over. Ordinary objects like vacuum cleaners, brooms, toys, and just about anything solid can cause damage to the surface. Think about who and what travels around the area where your aquarium is placed. You may want to think about having it near a highly active dog or a curious child (e.g., in their bedrooms) or busy hallways and entrance doors. Bottom line, make sure there is plenty of open space around your aquarium to avoid bumps, scrapes and difficulty moving around or past the fish tank.

Opt for a quiet space

While it is true that filters do release some amount of noise, excessive noise generated by devices such as speaker woofers can bother the fish. Sounds like this, or even sounds that comes from just tapping the glass of the aquarium, cause vibrations in the water, which can sound like a jets engine on the inside of the fish tank which can stress out your fish. Also, if you have shy fish, every time they hear any loud noise, they will scatter and hide, leaving you to stare at an empty tank. Placing the fish tank in a room with minimal noise would be better.

Decor or distraction?

Aquariums are a sight to behold, and that is a fact. Especially the saltwater aquariums since its content is much more robust. With this in mind, placing it next to the TV will do more distracting than focusing on what it is you are watching. Many have confessed that putting it next to the TV was a bad idea since they found themselves watching the fish in the aquarium most of the time instead of the TV. Along those lines, large fish tanks tend to grab the attention of the people in a room anyway. In a room where the tank should not be the focus, one might consider picking out a different location. However, if you do not mind the distraction, then by all means, enjoy your aquarium.

Keep in mind that while your fish's health and well being is important, you should also take into account your own needs as well. Aim to find a fish tank position that will give you the best view of your aquarium without posing any difficulties or risks to your fish's well being and the quality of your tank ecosystem. This advice may sound too rigid, but the aim is to save you from the trouble and heartache of losing fish or giving up entirely on fish keeping.

Interesting places/ideas to set up your aquarium:

- Kitchen Island with a built-in aquarium
- Aquarium house as a space separator
- A centerpiece for the living room
- Two in one aquarium and coffee table
- Aquarium house built into kitchen cabinets
- Custom modern aquarium built directly into the furniture
- Fill in empty space, e.g., under the stairs with a custom tank
- An aquarium mounted on a railing on the first floor of your home visible from the ground floor
- An aquarium wall

10. SELF-CLEANING FISH TANKS – PROS AND CONS

A self-cleaning aquarium sounds like the ultimate dream; no more hassles of rigorous cleaning that often prove to be stressful to both the fish and the aquarist. They are a gift to all those who crave to care for fish without the burden of constant water changes and the other recurring responsibilities that come with maintaining a fish tank, especially if you plan on gifting a child with an aquarium. However, even if you purchase a self-cleaning tank, you will still need to be responsible and look after your pet because owning a pet is a serious responsibility. Partial water changes will still be required to keep the environment safe for the fish.

It is important to keep in mind that most of these fish tanks come in small sizes, which as we have seen earlier, is not necessarily a good habitat for your fish. The smaller the tank, the more likely your fish will be stressed. The more stressed your fish is, the higher the chances for it to get aggressive or sick. Most experts consider self-cleaning tanks a lazy solution because one still needs to perform the necessary water parameter inspections.

Popular choices for these tanks are bettas, white cloud minnows, and shrimp. It is better to reserve ocean creatures for non aquaponic ponds, as most plants cannot live in saltwater. Overall, these tanks are suitable for both beginners and experts alike.

How self-cleaning fish tanks work

Most aquaponic systems are recirculating aquaculture systems, where water is recycled continuously through a series of interconnected fish tanks and waste treatment networks. These tanks work by using the aquaponics system, which is the combination of aquaculture (raising aquatic life) and hydroponics (growing plants without soil). In hydroponics, mineral nutrient solutions in a water solvent are used instead. An aquaponics setup consists of plants, aquatic life and bacteria which work together to create a balanced self cleaning environment. The waste products that come from the fish are used to fertilize the plants. In turn, the plants purify the water from the waste while the bacteria rid the water of ammonia and nitrates. The involvement of bacteria in this nitrogen cycle helps in making the environment a safe space for both the plants and the fish.

DIFFERNET TYPES OF SELF-CLEANING FISH TANKS

Gravity based self-cleaning fish tanks

They use a pump to siphon out dirty water from the bottom of the tank as you add clean water in at the top. This type of system is made so that it is strong enough to clean but not strong enough to suck your fish out. A good example of this is the "My Fun Fish Tank", whose main downside, as with most types of self-cleaning tanks, is its small size. Here, one needs to pour in clean water with a container placed by the pump to catch the dirty water.

Water garden tanks

This is basically an aquarium with a small garden growing at the top. An excellent example of this is the "Back to the Roots" self-cleaning tank or the "AquaSprouts" fish tank, which are excellent choices for beginners since they are easy to set up. Such tanks are also made for those that want to grow their own microgreens and herbs indoors.

Pros

Time savings

Self-cleaning aquariums save a lot of time, especially if you are a person with a very busy schedule. Also, if you are a person who tends to forget cleaning the tank, then this might be the best option for you. They do not require you to set aside time to engage in really protracted cleaning sessions like their counterpart tanks.

Proper filtration systems

Such aquariums tend to have integrated 3-stage filters, which provide the biological, mechanical, and chemical filtration needed to keep your aquarium safe, and minimize the amount of time you need to clean and change the water. Proper filtration encourages the growth of beneficial bacteria, reducing the risk of encountering a toxic ammonia spike.

Easier to clean than a regular tank

An aquarist with a self-cleaning tank will end up spending a minimal amount of time since most of these tasks are usually quite small, and a good part of the cleaning process is already 'automated.' In some cases, there is no need to change the filter at all, and for most, filters can be changed after only four weeks.

Low power consumption
Aquaponics use less power to run their systems since they are much smaller than the larger aquariums; hence will consume much less power, saving you a ton in electricity bills. The five main contributors to electrical energy usage in the system are water heaters, air blowers, box fans, a pump, and lights in the winter for seedling germination. The electricity used to power pumps and filters is microscopic compared to the larger tanks.

One can grow their own herbs
These tanks give owners the benefit of growing their own herbs at home while simultaneously enjoying being an aquarist. The benefit of this is that your herbs will not be contaminated by chemicals since they will grow naturally and organically. The herbs, once mature, can be harvested and eaten.

Great teaching tool for kids
Due to their simple nature, they act as a great tool to introduce children, both at home and school, to the aquarist life. Anyone looking to begin their journey of fish keeping on a much smaller scale to learn the ropes, before moving on to the larger tanks, can learn with these tanks. The best part is they look beautiful as decor in a room or as an office desk.

Cons

They might not work as advertised

Most self-cleaning tank reviews scream of broken parts and false advertisement. Relying on them 100% to clean the fish tank could make you end up with dead fish, so it is wise to continually check up on them and make sure everything is in check. Do not put all your faith in this system.

A tad too small

Fish need room to move, and when the space is too limiting, a lot of complications may arise. Keeping a fish tank below 3 gallons might even be considered animal cruelty by some. The little fish in tanks are likely to die much sooner than they would in a properly sized aquarium with a filtration device and heater. They are stuck in a tight, low-oxygen atmosphere with little space to do much of anything, even if they don't die. Examples of such fish tanks are the Penn-Plax and the EcoQube.

Fast buildup of toxic waste

A small volume of water means toxic ammonia and nitrite builds up much faster, and there isn't enough water to dilute the waste. The difference between humans and fish is that fish have to live with the toxic waste they produce. Just take a moment to imagine if you were placed into a confined area with no escape from your own waste. That is the daily life of fish, so the bigger the tank, the better.

Potentially unstable water parameters

Having a limited amount of water means any changes in pH or temperature will increase your fish's chances of stress. Stress triggers a fight or flight response in fish resulting in changes in their bodies. A hormone is secreted from the adrenal gland increasing their blood sugar, giving them massive amounts of energy. However, the hormones released by the adrenal gland inhibit the inflammatory response, which is intended to help your fish fight against disease.

Thanks to a shift in minters' metabolism, the water balance in your fish is disturbed, triggering freshwater fish to absorb and overhydrate excess water. This disturbance increases the energy required to control osmoregulation (capability to regulate body fluids). Breathing slows, blood pressure rises, and blood cells in reserve are released into the bloodstream. Their energy storage will be exhausted, further hormone imbalances will occur, and their immune systems will be significantly suppressed, increasing their risk of disease. The scary part is that you may not notice as these changes are happening since the fish will continue to act normal.

It's not all self-cleaning

Self sustaining aquariums still require heaters and food. The plants take care of filtration, but an aquarium heater is still needed to regulate the water temperature. The tank may be self-cleaning, but the feeding of the fish still happens as usual. Also, one still needs to perform 50% of the water changes every 2-3 days. Since the space is small, the waste build-up happens even faster; hence the water changes so the cleanings might need to happen more frequent than the regular fish tanks.

"Hacks" To Clean Your Tank

1. Set an alarm to remind you to change the water
2. Use an aquarium water test kit once a week to check your tank parameters
3. Use a gravel vacuum when performing water changes
4. Save time with a DIY water exchange system
5. Consider planting some hornwort plants in your tank
6. Make your own magnetic algae scrubber to clean your tank walls
7. Soak dirty tank decorations in a weak bleach solution
8. Add a reminder on your phone to replace the filter as needed
9. Use an aquarium safe lime cleaner to clean aquarium glass and fixtures
10. Soak your fishnets in a disinfecting solution

When buying an aquaponics fish tank, consider the following factors:

Surface area
To help with better oxygen absorption, get a tank that has a large top but a short bottom.

Cover
This is to prevent the fish from jumping out of the tank. Also, they do not require much light, and that is one of the reasons why fish tanks (some) come with lids.

Shape

This factor can be based on your preference. Round tanks are chosen for their effectiveness because the fish can swim easier, and the water can flow easier too. Waste rarely sticks in the corners of circular tanks, but all in all, this is usually a matter of preference.

Material
As mentioned, you can find glass or acrylic aquaponic tanks. You can compare your options and see which best works for you. In addition, you should find one that is waterproof, heavy-duty, sturdy, and one that can handle water pressure.

Size
Many of these aquaponics tanks are perfect for the indoors because they are small and compact, and will have a wider variety of placement options as opposed to the larger tanks. Try investing in a tank at least 3 gallons or more to ensure you keep your fish healthy.

Most of these tanks can be found on Amazon, e-Bay, or even a local pet store. However, if you do decide to go with the self-cleaning fish tank, here are a few well rated tanks you can start with:

- Marineland Contour Glass Aquarium kit
- biOrb Flow Aquarium
- AquaSprouts Garden
- Springworks Microfarm Aquaponic Garden
- Marineland Portrait Aquarium
- Ecolife ECO – Cycle Aquaponics indoor Gardening system
- EcoQubeC Aquarium

- Aquaponic Self-Cleaning Fish Tank By Penn Plax
- Fluval Spec III Aquarium kit
- Self-Cleaning Water Garden By Back To The Roots

There are also a range of online tutorials for designing and customizing your own aquaponics setup, so if you're looking to customize anything to your particular tank and lifestyle, this choice may be best for you. So what's the big takeaway here? Self-cleaning aquariums still require maintenance to keep both plants and fish alive.

11. HOW AN AUTOMATIC FISH FEEDER WORKS

An automatic fish feeder is designed to dispense the right amount of food into your aquarium at a specific time each day. This can be especially useful if you tend to forget to feed your fish or if you are planning on travelling. It can be set to dispense the food just once or more than once a day. Automatic fish feeders come in handy too for busy people with little time to spare. Since it is recommended that one feed their fish at the same time every day, these feeders can do just that. Most of them come in transparent plastic containers and can run for six weeks without having to be refilled. If you keep fish in a pond, there are models out there for you too.

They sit at the side or the top of the tank and consist of three main parts, namely: a hopper, a timer and a method to set the portion sizes. The hopper is the part that is filled with the food. The timer rotates the hopper in the process of dispensing the food. These devices can either be powered by batteries or power cords, depending on the type one buys. Some have suction cups that sit on the outside wall of the aquarium while others have mounting brackets that hook over the side of the tank.

With recent advancements in technology, some devices can be controlled using a mobile device by establishing a WiFi or Bluetooth connection with the source. Some models with a 'feed now' button drop the food outside the scheduled time. This can be useful when testing out whether or not the feeder actually works. Feeders also need to be maintained and cleaned, but doing so is not a burdensome task. It takes just a minute or two and can be done when doing your routine tank cleaning. It is paramount to ensure that the food is dry to prevent malfunctioning of the device. This means you can only use dry foods with a feeder. If your fish require a diet of live or frozen foods like bloodworms, perhaps you could switch to freeze dried foods or a different species of fish that will make the process easier for you.

An automatic feeder is not a necessity but a situational necessity, and to some, a luxury. One of the best times for aquarists to spend time with the fish is feeding time, and if you want to enjoy this privilege, then this device does nothing for you. An automatic fish feeder is there for your fish when you aren't. It is also a better alternative to leaving the feeding of your fish to a relative or a friend since they may accidentally end up overfeeding the fish.

Common types of automatic fish feeders

Rotating barrel fish feeders
This is the most common type of fish feeder. Simply fill the device with food, set the timer, and when feeding time rolls around, the food is automatically dropped into the fish tank. The amount of food dispensed is determined by the opening size of the barrel, but luckily you have control over that too. By adjusting the opening, you can decide whether the fish will have an entrée sized meal or a main course. Just make sure you do not over feed your fish while experimenting with this feature. A rotating barrel fish feeder holds the most amount of food, so if you are planning on travelling for an extended period, this is the best option as it can hold food for up to six weeks.

These feeders are less suitable for community tanks because sinking pellets and fish flakes can't be evenly dispensed since there's a single compartment. One type of fish food per rotating barrel fish feeder works best. Big crisps, algae wafers and sticks can become stuck in the opening, so this type of feeder is not suitable for large sized foods.

Portion control fish feeders
Think of this fish feeder as a pill container. You can fill each part with your fish's favorite type of food, and when dispensing time arrives, the feeder releases the food in that specific single portion into the tank then moves on to the next section next time. One can not only perfectly measure out each fish meal, but they can also mix different types of fish food, making sure all the different fish species needs in your tank are taken care of. You can mix up the food however you like, or place each tray with a specific type of food, e.g., one tray with pellets and the other with flakes and set them to release at different times throughout the day.

There is however a major drawback, the portion control feeders tend to hold less food than the barrel feeders. Some can come with up to 14 compartments meaning that feeding can last for two weeks with a session a day of food dispensing. If you feed more than once a day, that two week timeline significantly comes down. They also tend to take up more space and demand more rigorous cleaning than the barrel type. This automated fish feeder is also not suitable for small foods such as beta pellets due to the way the tray mechanism functions.

It is recommended that one choose an automatic fish feeder with a built in ventilation fan to prevent moisture from building up and keeping the food dry. The downside of this is that the fan only runs while the food container is turning, which is about ten seconds. Some might argue that ten seconds of air is better than none. Some models like the Fish Mate F14 allow you to attach an air line tubing from an air pump to continuously blow air over the food, effectively eliminating moisture and condensation. When you have moisture issues, push your automatic fish feeder further from the waterline. Additionally, consider switching to pellets if you use flakes, they do not absorb moisture at the same rate as flaked foods.

Using an automatic feeder means entrusting the life of your fish to the machine. If it fails, your fish starve and die off. If it overfeeds, you run the risk of ammonia spikes. That's why you want the best automatic fish feeder on the market, not only to keep your fish full but safe too. When choosing one, opt for these tried and tested feeders:

- Eheim Everyday Fish Feeder (Offers the best value for your money.)
- Fish Mate F14 (Best for mixed foods and measured amounts)
- Lifegard Aquatics Intelli-Feed (Best for humid environments)
- Sera Feed A Plus
- Zoo Med BettaMatic
- Hydor Automatic Fish Feeder

Helpful tips

1. Test the feeder to make sure it works before going on vacation
2. Secure the feeder using clamps to avoid accidents
3. Don't place your feeder too close to the overflow or the filter outlet

There are quite a few automatic fish feeders available in the market, so when choosing one, consider the following factors:

1. Choose one with the 'feed now' button to be able to test out the functionality of the device when need be as opposed to waiting for hours on end until feeding time arrives.
2. A feeder with a built-in memory remembers the feeding times previously set even with the batteries removed, unlike the rest.
3. Opt for a feeder with the option of dispensing food multiple times a day for flexibility purposes.
4. A feeder with multiple mounting options means that you do not have to buy a new automatic fish feeder when you make a tank upgrade.
5. A built-in fan is better than no fan at all.

Some cheap models malfunction easily or allow moisture to get into the feeder. Look for fish feeders that will allow the moisture to escape. If you decide to invest in one, then it's safer to pay a higher price for a device that will keep your fish safe and healthy if you are absent for a long period of time.

12. THE ABCs OF FISH TANK THERMOMETERS

While heaters are wonderful for regulating your water temperatures, they are not always 100% accurate. Having a separate thermometer can help you track and adjust your fish tank's temperature accordingly. Relying on a thermometer that isn't accurate is just as effective as having none at all. You can't check the water temperature by just looking at it. Checking your thermometer when you feed your fish or after water changes is an easy way to spot any issues with temperature early.

Some aspects to consider when choosing an aquarium:

1. **Thermometer type (these come in three types)**

a) Liquid-filled thermometers - they resemble the traditional mercury bulb thermometers but are filled with a less dangerous liquid than mercury. Some float/sink/sit inside the tank or come with a suction cup.

- Submersible aquarium thermometer – as the name suggests, are submerged in the tank and sit there, giving you a hands free alternative to measure the temperature by peeking inside the tank through the glass. They are mostly made from glass and work best in a large tank. Submersible thermometers are the cheapest kind but are not recommended if you have aggressive fish.

- Floating submersible thermometer – these thermometers are barely practical since they spin around with even the slightest water movement, and the only way to read them is from the front. Due to the movement, they can get pushed around a lot, and the decor and plants in the tank might inhibit one from reading them clearly.

- Standing submersible thermometer – these are weighted thermometers that sink and stand at the bottom of the tank. If your fish bumps your standing thermostat, then you'll have to dunk your hand inside your tank to set it back up.

- Suction cup submersible thermometer - Upon securing the suction cup to your aquarium's window, you can rest assured that the next time you check the temperature, your thermometer will be in the same position. You can move and attach it wherever you please, making this one of the best thermometers to use. Instead of suction cups, some use magnets while others hang from the edge of your aquarium.

b) Digital thermometers - A probe is attached inside the tank while the display unit sits outside of the tank. Some modern models can even come with alarms that alert you when the temperature falls below or above the desired range. Digital thermometers are made of plastic, so you don't have to worry about breaking a glass thermometer inside your aquarium. If you want a thermometer that does not permanently sit in your aquarium, this is your best choice. They come as either fixed or wired thermostats but are also the most expensive type. When choosing a style, check the probe cord length, as it varies from model to model.

c) Adhesive strip thermometers – its thin profile allows you to stick it outside the tank to provide an approximate reading. Stick on thermometers are the most widely used thermometers in freshwater aquariums as they are often offered as part of a new aquarium kit. They are often referred to as LCD thermometers (liquid crystal display). The liquid changes color according to the temperature of your aquarium. The problem with these is that the temperature reading is also affected by the temperature of the room. So, if your room is hotter or colder than the water inside your aquarium, then the sticker can give you an incorrect reading. Most of them also fail after one year.

2. Precision

A good quality thermometer will have a +/-2F degree accuracy; hence why most people recommend using a digital thermometer. The point of having a thermometer is to get one that gives an accurate reading. Look for a well calibrated model, more so if the fish you have need precise temperatures to survive.

3. Ease of reading

Digital thermometers featuring a large LCD are easy to read, particularly when you are not dealing with any eyesight problems.

4. Power options

Some models need AAA batteries which are easy to find and reasonably priced. Others need less common batteries like the CR2032 that are, on the other hand, more reliable and less corrosion prone. Both adhesive strips and liquid filled thermometers require no operating batteries. The digital versions run on batteries full-time.

5. Lifespan

If you want an aquarium thermometer that lasts for a long time, be willing to pay the extra cash for it. Liquid filled models have to be rugged and tough, since they may harm the fish if they shatter inside the aquarium while the stick-on ones have a very short lifespan. Ultimately, it is up to you to decide what you think will work best for your specific type of fish tank.

A good recommendation would be the **Cooper Atkins Digital Pocket Thermometer**. The **JW Smarttemp** is also a great option for a submersible thermometer too. For the alarm types, you can also look at the Linkbird LTC. The sticker thermometer king, though not recommended, has to be LCR Hallcrest. It is important to balance the water temperatures between the freshwater and the water already present in the tank when making water changes.

Always use a thermometer to ensure that temperatures match until the water adjustments are made to prevent your fish and invertebrates from being too overworked by your heater.

Stable water temperatures will make the difference between a healthy tank and an aquarium that crashes overnight. Any drastic change in water temperature can make your fish more vulnerable to diseases like fin rot. Therefore, when thinking about the temperature of the fish tank, you should always bear in mind the room temperature. Even if you already have an aquarium thermometer in your fish tank, it might be a wise to use a different thermometer periodically to test whether the first thermometer still works and provides accurate readings. If you buy a classic mercury thermometer, you'll want one that's not likely to crack or break and is fully submergible. The digital versions tend to provide the most accurate reading.

13. LED AQUARIUM LIGHTING AND WHAT YOU NEED TO KNOW

People new to aquariums might easily be overwhelmed by the task of setting up and stocking your first fish tank. Many things go into starting up your aquarium, and functionality is one significant aspect to look at when picking out equipment. Choosing the right equipment may be puzzling to many people, but fear not, if you familiarize yourself with a few basic terms and concepts about Aquariums, you'll get the hang of it pretty quickly.

Lighting is one crucial aspect of aquariums not only for its decorative functionality but also because it helps the ecosystem thrive through photosynthesis and establishment of a day and night cycle, which is very important for the fish in the aquarium.

Functions of lighting in aquariums

i. Simulation of a true under water environment that is both healthy and aesthetically appealing.

ii. Influencing fish behavior - Lighting with higher blues stimulates feeding and mating behavior in your fish. Improper lighting will cause stress to the fish, thus making the fish more aggressive or lethargic.

iii. Lighting improves the health of the plants in the aquarium by promoting photosynthesis.

iv.   Establishing a day and night cycle - This helps create a proper sleep and feeding schedule for the fish, thereby promoting healthy growth.

v.   Decorative purposes - Lighting creates a visually appealing aquarium which attracts hobbyists.

vi.   Enhances warmth of the aquarium - As much aquariums come with temperature regulators, Lighting enhances the warmth of the aquarium and generally promotes the health of the fish.

There are different types of lighting that you can use for aquariums, and the diversity of light allows aquarium hobbyists to pick the kind of lighting that is suitable for the fish in the aquarium. We can categorize these types of lighting into four main categories:

i.   **LED (Light Emitting Diode) systems**- This lighting type consists of small diodes attached to a circuit board. They are becoming very popular due to being energy efficient and their ability to fit into a wider variety of fixtures. They also emit less heat than normal fluorescent and incandescent lighting.

ii.   **Normal output fluorescent lighting** - We also call this standard fluorescent lighting. They are easy to install and affordable, but they produce more heat than LED lighting and need to be replaced regularly.

iii. **High-intensity metal halide lighting** - These use high-intensity discharge (HID) lighting systems and are used in large aquariums to ensure maximum illumination. This type of lighting is easy to set up but can be expensive to run and produces a lot of heat, which can cause fluctuating temperatures in water.

iv.   **Compact fluorescent lighting** - These offer a higher light output than standard fluorescent lighting. It can incorporate dual or quad tubes in a single lighting fixture hence producing more light and saving space.

LED lighting is the most commonly used technology in almost all lighting products. LED lighting has the ability to save energy and look fancy at the same time. This has increased its popularity in the market as well.

With that in mind, let us look at the basics of LED lighting systems

What is LED, and how does it work?

LED stands for *Light-Emitting Diode.* How does LED work? An electrical current passes through a microchip, which illuminates the tiny light sources we call LEDs, and the result is visible light. LEDs are integrated into bulbs and fixtures for general lighting applications. LEDs are small in size and thereby provide unique design opportunities for producing fancier light bulbs and fixtures. LEDs can either be incorporated as permanent light sources in a light bulb, or a hybrid approach can be used where a non-traditional "bulb" or replaceable light source format is used and specially designed for a unique fixture.

LEDs and Heat

To prevent performance issues, LED lighting systems contain a heat sink that absorbs the heat produced by illumination. The heat sink then dissipates the heat into the surrounding environment. This helps prevent overheating and the burn out of LED bulbs. Higher heat in the LED system leads to light degradation and shortens the lifetime of LED bulbs.

Lifetime of LED Lighting Products

LED life ratings have to be measured differently than legacy lighting sources because the technology is just so much different than in other light sources. LED's typically do not fail like legacy lighting systems. Instead, their lumens depreciate, wherein the brightness of the LED dims slowly over time. Case in point, if the lifetime of an LED bulb is estimated to be 30,000 hours, after the 30,000 hours is over, the bulb will still light up but with less lighting impact.

Differences between led lighting and other sources of lighting

LED lighting differs from incandescent and fluorescent in a few different ways. If designed well, LED lighting is progressively proficient, flexible, and lasts much longer. LEDs are "directional" light sources, which implies they radiate light a particular way, in contrast to incandescent and fluorescent, which emanate light and warmth in every direction. That implies LEDs can utilize light productively in the direction that is needed.

Basic LED hues incorporate gold, red, green, and blue. To create white light, unique shading LEDs are consolidated or secured with a phosphor material that changes over the shade of the light to a natural "white" light utilized in homes. Phosphor is a yellowish material that covers a few LEDs. Hued LEDs are generally utilized as sign lights and marker lights, similar to lighted power button on a PC.

Incandescent bulbs emit light by heating a metal filament with electricity until it is "white" hot, or is said to incandesce. As a consequence, incandescent bulbs release heat as 90 percent of their energy. LEDs on the other hand have heat sinks that keep the lighting systems at an optimum temperature.

In a CFL, an electric flow streams between cathodes at each finish of a cylinder containing gases. This response produces bright (UV) light and warmth. The UV light is changed into noticeable light when it strikes a phosphor covering within the bulb.

Advantages of LED lighting systems over legacy lighting systems

1) **Longer lifespan** - The long lifetime is probably the most important advantage of LEDs compared to conventional lighting solutions. The average running time of an LED is 50,000 to 100,000 running hours or more. That is 2-4 times as long as most lights that are fluorescent, metal halide, and even sodium vapour. Less replacement implies less maintenance costs and less costs for replacement parts

86

2) **Safety** - Safety is probably the most often ignored benefit of LED lighting. The number one threat to lighting is heat emission. LEDs emit almost no forward heat, whereas conventional bulbs, such as incandescent bulbs, transform over 90 percent of the total energy used to power them into electricity directly. That means that only 10 percent of the incandescent lights that fuel energy are actually used for lighting. This makes incandescent lighting highly inefficient. In addition, since LEDs consume less power, they can work effectively on low-voltage electrical systems.

3) **Energy-efficient** - LEDs are our most energy efficient lighting system, they have an efficiency of 80-90 percent, meaning that 80-90 percent of their energy is converted into light rather than heat. Incandescent bulbs lose 80-90 percent of their energy as heat and therefore are only effective at 10-20 percent.

4) **Durability** - LEDs are made from very durable materials and components that can withstand harsh weather, shocks, vibrations and abrasions. For this purpose, they are increasingly being adopted for aquariums.

5) **Design flexibility** - Due to the small size of LED systems, LED light arrays can be positioned and combined to generate effective, but still controllable illumination in a limitless number of ways. The hue, shadow, brightness, and light delivery can be managed to perfection, making mood lighting not only technically useful, but also calming, elevating, and energizing.

6) **Ability to work in extreme temperatures** - LEDs are suitable for use in icy conditions, such as freezer rooms or extreme climates. Many lamps, such as incandescent or fluorescent, can be influenced by the cold, but even when the mercury drops, LEDs are reliable.

7) **Ability to work on low voltage power** - Since LEDs can operate with low voltage, they are reliable even when there are power issues in aquariums. This will ensure continuity of lighting benefits to the aquarium ecosystem.

8) **Instant powering on and off** - As in the case of metal halide lamps, there is no warm-up time. Furthermore, regular switching doesn't cause system degradation.

9) **LEDs are more environmentally safe** - LEDs contain no poisonous substances or mercury like components. They are also 100% recyclable; using LED lights will help you reduce a third of your carbon footprint. They also last 35 times longer than a halogen bulb on average meaning that they often save on material and production costs.

10) **Customizable light intensity** - LED lights can be dimmed and configured to allow natural sunset and sunrise dimming. This is especially good for nocturnal fish, as the tank can be left with a dim blue light to mimic moonlight and allow for feeding and viewing purposes. There are also strips of LED lighting that mimic the monthly lunar cycle.

Disadvantages of LED lighting systems in aquariums

1) **Availability** - Many aquarium kits that come with a lamp or hood do not provide LED lights. Popular combination units like the Eclipse systems are only available with regular fluorescent bulbs.

2) **Affordability** - LED attachments appear to be a little more expensive to buy upfront. The initial budget to purchase LED systems is larger, but it is made up for that over time in energy savings as well as in the costs of replacing bulbs.

3) **Limited use for Planted aquariums** - In the case of planted aquariums, another primary weakness is most LED systems don't have the correct levels that are best for aquarium plants.

Light intensity and spectrum for aquariums

Light differs in intensity from one source to another. Spectrum is a way to describe the mixture of different colors or wavelengths produced by a light. A Kelvin rating or "K rating" is also given to the light spectrum. Light sources giving off a yellowish or warm effect have a low Kelvin rating, whereas those emitting a clear bluish white or cool light have a high Kelvin rating. Most aquarium freshwater lights are rated between 5,500 and 8,000 Kelvin.

Intensity and spectrum are far less relevant in aquariums or with artificial plants, although some lights are better than others for natural colors. A light that is too intense can promote algae, particularly in tanks that are not planted. When it comes to live plants, proper strength and range will differentiate between success and failure of a tank. Other wavelengths, especially blue, penetrate deeper into the water than others, and this may be crucial for plants to live on.

Algae and how light affects it

A popular belief in keeping aquariums is that too much light induces excessive growth in algae. Algae are the purification of water by definition and are a regular part of every aquarium. The reality is that phosphorus build-up triggers nuisance algae outbreaks more frequently than lighting issues. Plant aquarium owners never have to clean algae even though they use high production lighting because the plants use nutrients to avoid any algae. The key to avoiding algae growth is to control nutrients with frequent changes in water, chemical filter media, providing the right amount of light, and not to over feed your fish.

The word "nutrients" in aquariums refers to nitrate and phosphate, which usually comes from fish food and the resulting fish waste. There is another source that is water from the tap. Many tap water supplies contain high levels of these impurities, and water changes with nitrate or water charged with phosphate will not reduce levels, and may even cause them to increase. If your tap water contains high levels of nutrients, using reverse osmosis or deionized water with the addition of Aqueon Water Renewal to fill your tank will help. Finding the right light for your aquarium boosts its stunning beauty and guarantees your fish, plants and invertebrates long-term health!

14. FISH TANK GRAVEL: CHOICES AND VARIETY

The underlying layer of an aquarium, also known as substrate, can be gravel or sand. It is important not only for esthetic reasons but also for the health and well-being of your fish and plants. Depending on the plants and animals that you keep in your aquarium you may have strong preferences for the substrate you will use. The common substrates for aquariums are:

- Gravel - This substrate comes in particles ranging from 2mm-5mm (about ¼ inch in size). It can be very decorative because of the range of materials used to make gravel. It is the most preferred substrate for freshwater aquariums because it allows water to flow through it, preventing the build-up of amoebas and bacteria in the substrate.

- Sand - Labeled the most natural substrate since most aquarium fish come from an environment with sand, silt or mud, all of which are replicated precisely by sand. Sand contains little or no gaps between each grain, which means that there's nowhere that food and poop can get stuck, making sand one of the easiest substrates to keep clean.

- Pebbles - These are large substrate particles ranging from 6mm-64mm (up to 2 ½ inches).

Although very beautiful and decorative, the large gaps between pebbles can be toxic to your fish because food that drops in the gaps attracts bacteria that produces nitrites which are poisonous to fish.

- Soil - Mostly used in planted aquariums to promote the growth of plants. The soil used in aquariums is a little different from the normal muddy soil. Substrate soil from your local fish store is specifically designed to prevent it from mixing with water while also providing sufficient nutrients for your plants to grow.

Benefits of using aquarium gravel

1) Decorative purposes - Gravel can help to accentuate other decorations, conceal equipment, anchor items or plants, and display your fish. Gravel might also help to disguise the debris that accumulates in your tank every day far better than if the bottom was empty.

2) Simulation of natural underwater environment - Aquarium gravel can help create an atmosphere that is more suitable for your fish. This substrate provides a haven for eggs to be laid that otherwise would be eaten by adult fish. The gravel also becomes a home to good bacteria that breaks down fish waste.

3) Anchors Plants - This is the perfect way to anchor any aquarium plants which you add to your fish

tank. When put in gravel, your plants can root and grow in the right conditions.

Preparing gravel for your fish tank

When choosing this sort of substratum, you'll want to use a gravel designed explicitly for aquarium use. Aquarium gravel is chemically inert, unlike ordinary gravel you find on the streets. This will stop bedding from altering the water chemistry.

Another distinction is that gravel that is specially built to be used in your tank would be finer in texture than other gravels. Not only does this smooth texture mimic the bedding you'd expect to find in a body of water, but it's also better for fish.

A practice used by most aquarium keepers is that they start a two inch depth of gravel at the base of your freshwater tank. Most owners will raise depth to three or more inches toward the back of the aquarium. The created incline allows for more choices when aquascaping, and also provides more surface area for use by beneficial bacteria.

You'll want to rinse it after you buy your gravel before bringing it into your aquarium. The kit may contain dust, dirt, and other forms of debris or contaminants which may be harmful to your fish. Preliminary cleaning of the gravel prevents certain contaminants from reaching the water column. The method requires the use of a sieve that is put over a seal. Placing the gravel in the sieve, you simply run water over it while shaking the sieve until there is clear water flowing out into the container. You must continue this cycle until all the bedding gravel in the tank has been washed. Do not rinse gravel over your drain, since some gravel can slip out of the sieve.

Basic cleaning by vacuuming the gravel should be performed regularly. The process involves the use of a gravel vacuum, which removes debris off the substratum by siphoning water into a bucket through a hose.

Types of gravel

If you are searching for the best gravel aquarium color to make your fish stand out, or you want to find one that's good for plants, there's gravel out there to suit your needs. Aquarium gravel is available in all shapes, sizes, colors and sets. Below are a few types of gravel that you can consider using in your fish tank:

I.   Plain Black or White Gravel - Since its plain colored, it will definitely improve your fish's color and make it stand out in the aquarium.

II.   Creek Stone Gravel - It consists of small colorful stones with a natural look effect. The natural elegance of the stones brings more appeal to your aquarium.

III. Coated Glofish Gravel - This gravel comes coated in vibrant colors that enhance the mood in your fish tank.

IV.   Large vs Small Gravel - The main difference between larger and smaller gravel is that larger particles create a greater distance between individual particles that allows room for biological waste and residual food waste to fall in between and build up, which could potentially be hazardous to the fish if not properly cleaned.

15. CHOOSING WI-FI CAMERAS FOR YOUR FISH TANK

A Wi-Fi Camera is a small camera that links to your home wireless network, and it broadcasts live video feeds to every mobile device, laptop or computer anywhere in the world anytime anyone logs in. Having Surveillance cameras for your fish tank is a good investment because this will enable you to monitor your fish even when you are not around. The cameras can also help you store information that will help investigate any problem that might come up in the aquarium. They are also important if you have a tank sitter, you can track them, or just walk through what you want them to do.

For the installation of Wi-Fi cameras, you can either use a technician or do it yourself. All you need to do is plug it into the wall for power, connect it to your home Wi-Fi network, attach the device to your phone/tablet/desktop, and you can access the live stream securely from anywhere in the world.

Many of the common models are either fixed cameras that you install and point to your desired view, or you can buy one that comes on a controllable base. The controllable ones allow you to click, pan and zoom the camera remotely, allowing you to look at several objects.

Features of Wi-Fi cameras

1. 1080p Full HD for High Quality Video Streaming.
2. Infra-Red Night Vision - This improves video quality even in low light.
3. Motion Detection - Enables alerts in case of an abnormality.
4. 2-Way Voice Communication to help communicate with a tank sitter.
5. Global Access to Video Stream - This ensures you can access surveillance from anywhere in the world.
6. Pan/Tilt/Zoom of Camera - This allows more control as you can view the fish tank from different angles.
7. Notification of Motion via App - This ensures real-time alerts get to you to make timely responses.
8. Cloud Storage for Recording - Records are important for reference purposes.
9. Multiple Mounting Options - This provides flexibility during installation.
10. Simple Setup - This helps hobbyists do installations themselves, thereby saving labor costs.
11. Security features - Some cameras come with features that allow you to set up passwords to avoid unauthorized access. Some even allow multi-factor authentication for even better security.

Steps for installing camera

Installing your Wi-Fi camera is usually a straightforward process which can be completed with ease by even the least technically minded. Here are some installation tips that can help:

1. **Mounting The Camera** - Find a place to install your camera where it will be out of the way and will not get knocked around when maintaining the aquarium. In case of privacy issues, try not to set up the camera from across the room looking at the tank.

2. **Powering up The Camera** - Most cameras would only need to plug their power into the wall. For those powered by a home phone, make sure you have convenient access to uninstall the charging plug. Start up the camera according to the instructions for installation.

3. **Connecting to Your Home Wi-Fi Network -** It's normally a very easy process, and every camera manufacturer has simple instructions on how to do it. The most popular approach today is to install the App and then wait for the camera to be found on your Bluetooth or Wi-Fi devices list.

4. **Test The Camera -** To ensure that the camera and software are set up correctly, check the video stream to your device and web browser.

5. **Focus The Camera -** Most cameras will have a digital focus or ring on the lens, which will need to

be changed to ensure the sharpest quality of the image.

6. **Adjust The Camera Settings -** In case you have a saltwater fish tank, you will need to adjust camera settings. Saltwater aquariums produce a lot of blue light in the color spectrum, and the color settings of the camera's, in particular the 'White Balance' will need to be changed to get the color set right. The camera user manual should provide good instructions on how to do this.

7. **Security -** When all camera settings have been completed, now is the time to set up the video feed to make sure all security options are enabled, including creating a strong username and password that's hard to hack.

Top brands for aquarium Wi-Fi cameras

The list below contains top brands for Wi-Fi cameras that are usable for fish tanks:

1. Nest Indoor Camera
2. Netgear Arlo
3. Wyze Cam
4. Amcrest Surveillance Camera
5. Wansview Wireless Pet Camera
6. Ring Indoor Camera
7. AUTOAQUA Qeye and QShooter.

16. THINGS YOU NEED TO KNOW ABOUT FISH TANK STANDS AND CABINETS

A stand is an integral part of many aquariums. Aquarium stands come in many forms, sizes and materials. When looking for the right stand, attention must be given to the features of your aquarium. An effective stand that is both durable and solid will accommodate a heavier and larger tank. The stand's strength should be in line with the aquarium's gallon capacity. In addition, there are a few stands that are specially built to accommodate tanks that come with bow-shaped fronts as well as rectangular in form.

There are several different kinds of materials to consider when purchase an aquarium stand.

Common materials include:

- MDF Particle board - The least expensive alternative is particle board. It is the wood material which is often used to create branded stands. While inexpensive particle board is not suitable for maintaining saltwater aquariums. Wood does not blend well with humidity, and if exposed to it, will decay pretty quickly. If you hire a carpenter to build your stand, or you are familiar with woodworking and know how to paint and seal it, MDF might be a good alternative if you're on a budget.

- Plywood - Plywood is the traditional material option and has been used by several higher end brands. This is much sturdier than MDF and is mostly used to build furniture and cabinets. Plywood is a good choice for a more durable material which is designed to last and sustain more massive tanks. Plywood is often the material used to construct higher end kitchen cabinets. It's stainable, and you can create a custom look with many veneers. They can be painted or sealed and will stand the test of time.

- Metal - Larger aquariums come with metal support hardware. Metal offers exceptional structural strength, capable of holding greater weights over time without suffering any damage. Metal frames are typically made of aluminum or stainless steel. Aluminum is particularly common outside of the U.S., but is gaining popularity in the U.S. because it is lightweight. A stand made from T-Slot Aluminum Framing Systems is especially useful to those who are trying to create a design for a large aquarium, but keep in mind it can be very costly.

Keeping in mind the humidity of your tank is important for your stand's durability. Your aquarium stand needs to have ample space to store your equipment. For example, reef aquariums need significant amount of equipment. Tanks with wide door openings and ample space will help you conceal this equipment, safeguarding your tank's beauty. If you'd like to get a sump in your tank, you will have to take into account the space it would take up when you're looking for a stand.

If you want to maintain a clean aquarium, it is prudent to buy a tank with concealable storage and holes in the backboard to feed the wires through. If you're a novice aquatic hobbyist or are likely to want to change the location of your tank at some point in the future, you're probably better off purchasing an easy-install tank stand. East setup is a consideration that is often underestimated and can cause many problems if not accounted for. Some stands come with metal to metal cam fittings that could be slightly more difficult than wooden screws to assemble.

The height of your stand impacts your aquarium's visibility and accessibility. If you have a small tank with a few fish species, you'll want a tall stand that will make it much easier for you to see and communicate with your pets. Stands with adjustable feet can be purchased too. This function can be useful if you want your tank to be elevated or lowered, depending on its environment.

You'll find a wide range of pricing options when shopping for an aquarium stand. When it comes to a saltwater aquarium and larger freshwater aquariums, you need to take into account the value of efficiency.

Let's look at the four different types of stand for comparison purposes:

- **Standard Aquarium Stands** - You will typically find a regular aquarium stand in a general pet store or online. They're usually made from MDF and particle board. Many of these stands are made at the lowest possible price. While they can operate in a freshwater setup or no sump setups, they will, in the long run not meet the needs of a saltwater tank or larger freshwater aquarium. The explanation for this is that if the stand is mounted with a sump, the high humidity generated from the sump inside the tank will cause warping from inside the stand. For these reasons, I do not suggest a regular aquarium stand for a saltwater or larger freshwater system from the general pet stores. There is obviously too much money in your tank system to ruin it by going cheap on a stand.

- **Brand Name Stands** - Brand name stands are furniture usually manufactured by high-end manufacturers who specialize in making hobbyist stands. The closest example of these stands will be the stands you'll find in all-in-one aquarium installations. Such stands are well built with a frame made of wood or metal (typically aluminum or stainless steel). They are usually built with plywood instead of MDF, if they are wood. These also have flexibility that suits the hobby (storage shelves, cable ports, etc.)

- **Custom Built Stands** - A stand is usually designed by manufacturers of custom aquariums or brand names that specialize in high-end buildings. They are the most costly types of aquarium stands and are typically made to order. They can be made of wood or metal. Usually, they will be equipped with custom cabinet doors and shelves to match the aquarium requirements. These are of outstanding quality but ideal for a high-end budget.

- **DIY Stand** - Many hobbyists that are also skilled with DIY projects can create their own aquarium stands with the exact features, dimensions and overall look they want. Below are tips for DIY fish tank stands;

    I. Make sure the stand frame supports the entire edge of the aquarium.

    II. Make sure the wood is directly in contact with wood from the floor straight up to the aquarium.

    III. Connect the frame with wood screws and wood glue together.

    IV. Assemble your flooring stand frame, which should be level and square.

    V. Always put a ½ to 1" thick rigid foam between the aquarium and the stand.

    VI. Design the height of your stand carefully, so that you can fit all the equipment inside the stand.

    VII. Double test the size/opening of the doors to ensure that all the equipment you want to fit through the doors in the stand.

Generally, stands are open at the top. Although this will work well for glass aquariums, if it's made from acrylic, you'll need to support the entire bottom of the tank. It is recommended that you purchase a self-levelling mat for rimless aquariums. This is because the wood can create pressure points within the glass in a rimless aquarium. Many manufacturers will provide the necessary support for an acrylic and rimless tank. It is good to have an opening at the top if you are going to put a substantially sized sump in it because it would be difficult to move the aquarium stand once your tank has found a place in your home that works.

Canopies in fish tanks are beginning to become less popular these days with the introduction of rimless aquariums and mounted lighting systems on the ceilings and tanks. It really comes down to personal preference though. Not buying a canopy will save you some money, but a lot of hobbyists still use it.

17. FISH TANK ORNAMENTS AND ACCESSORIES

You'll need to have some ornaments and plants to keep your aquatic pets happy. Fish need plants and ornaments in the tank to hide and feel safe among themselves. There's something to match every aquatic home, from natural rocks and wooden ornaments to vibrant plants and fun themed hideaways. Deciding on your fish tank decor can be a frustrating process, especially for less creative people. Below are tips for the things you need to consider for aquarium decoration and accessories.

Things to consider when picking aquarium accessories and ornaments

The Size of Your Aquarium

The size of our fish tank should be a big consideration because you don't want to under-decorate, and you don't want to overcrowd your fish tank with too many accessories. If your fish have no place to run around, it'll be pretty distressing for your fish too.

When you have a smaller tank, it's easier to have one or two attractive decorations that stand out instead of several that leave little living space for your pets. You can go with decorations like sunken ships, mermaid kingdoms, or similar accessories with a specific theme.

Here's how to get the proper height for your aquarium accessories:

Divide your tank into three zones: top, middle and bottom. Fish prefer to spend much of their time in each of these three regions, so it is important to have some free space in each one.

To divide the available space equally, it's prudent to have one or two tall objects growing up into the top zone (depending on the size of your aquarium) and then two or three short ones about one or two inches from the bottom of your tank.

When your decorations follow some kind of pattern or theme, your fish will feel better and safer. Following these decoration and accessory tips can help with the theme integration without making your fish feel awkward.

The Color of Your Fish
When you're worried about messing with your aquarium's beauty, you can prevent this by considering your fish's color. Your decoration color will either enhance or clash with your fish. When you have plenty of lightly colored fish, a dark substratum and bland decorations will help complement those colors. Vibrant, colorful fish look amazing against white gravel and pale decorations, making the fish color pop on a colorless backdrop.

Natural vs Wild Aquarium Theme
The color of your ornaments and accessories will set your aquarium theme. If you want your tank to have a natural looking theme, green plants are excellent choices in terms of color. Neon colors and vivid colors will produce a wilder, flashier look and help draw attention to different areas of your aquarium. When you've decided on a theme, carefully choose the color of your decorations and accessories to match your tank's look.

How Active Are Your Fish?

Highly active fish have a significantly higher intake of oxygen than more inactive species. If you have these fish, oxygen producing decorations such as bubble chests and underwater rivers and bridges will help keep your fish safe and keep them active too.

Sharp Edges

Often times, decorations such as fake plants may have sharp edges, and may scratch at their scales, causing bruises or even infections which can seriously affect your fish. When choosing accessories for your aquarium, make sure you avoid any that have sharp edges. Bottom line is you want to create an appealing look for your fish tank without endangering the health of your fish.

Focal Points

When you add decorations and accessories to your fish tank, choosing one or two focal points will help. Things such as mermaid statues and bridges attract the attention of people, set the scene in your aquarium and compliment your overall design.

Safety of Non-Commercial Items

If you're adding a toy or anything plastic to your fish tank, you'll have to make sure no nasty chemicals spill into your tank. Keep them in the tank for a couple of days, and then check the water to make sure there are no unnecessary parameter adjustments. You should never add something that is not explicitly planned for aquatic decoration, without first quarantining it.

Different styles of aquarium decor to inspire you

It is essential to recognize the advantages and possible disadvantages of each when selecting which decorations to add to your aquarium.

i. Driftwood

Natural driftwood is a common addition to many aquariums and can help to create a simple, natural feeling. It also serves as a great hiding place for shy fish. Driftwood can be bought in many pet shops and is typically very clean. However, you can fish driftwood from rivers and streams, and add it to your tank as well.

When doing this, you should exercise patience, and be sure to quarantine the wildwood. If you don't, you run the risk of introducing dangerous microbes and parasites into your fish tank, with the potential to cause serious illness or death to your fish. Driftwood will sometimes take quite some time to sink. One way to accelerate it is by digging a few holes in it.

ii. Plants

In many aquariums, the plants are a ubiquitous decoration. Many people like it because it adds color to the tank. Some include them because plants are present in many ecosystems with freshwater and can give the tank a more natural look. If you go to the pet shop, you can see a wide variety of options when it comes to aquarium plants.

iii. Caves

Caves will add an exotic, natural look to your aquarium, creating an attraction for fish to swim under and connect with. Many hobbyists suggest introducing objects for certain fish to hide under for protection while holding prey, and at the same time serving as enticing hiding place for these species. While the natural rocks found in the wild can be used as caves, these rocks should be boiled for at least one hour before they are introduced to your tank, destroying any harmful microbes and parasites.

PVC piping may also be used, just be sure to quarantine any plastics before applying them in your tank to ensure that they are secure and that no chemicals are leaking out.

iv.   Ships

Sunken ships are a healthy, fish-friendly choice that complements most tank designs if you are looking to build a natural sea-like theme. Ships also have great hiding spots for fish, allowing prey species to cover up for protection and comfort.

v.   Ruins

Ancient ruins provide an excellent addition to Atlantis mermaid themed tanks, and serve as ideal places to hide prey fish. When adding ruins of any sort, be sure they are designed for that purpose, and make sure they have been safely quarantined or decontaminated prior to use.

vi.   Statues

In sea themed aquariums, human and animal sculptures look fantastic, serving as glamorous decoration choices adding an imaginative and unique feel to an otherwise standard aquarium. When purchasing more towering figures, make sure they don't clutter your tank, and most importantly follow the design and style guidelines described above.

vii.   Aquarium Backgrounds

The aquarium background will serve as an ideal centerpiece for your fish tank. All poster backgrounds, layered 3D, and textured backgrounds can be used to create a more natural and imaginative look for your aquarium.

viii.   Submersible Light Ornament

You may also attach submersible lights to fish tanks, which provide a soft, enticing glow without being too bright and intrusive for fish. They serve as a perfect way to make your aquarium vivid without upsetting your pets. Submersive lights can also come in a variety of colors, enabling you to change the aesthetics and improve different tones of color.

ix.   Ceramic Ornaments

Introducing ceramic ornaments into an aquarium is a controversial activity. Some hobbyists say that it is perfectly healthy and others are strongly opposed to its use. The reality is that some ceramic ornaments are, in fact totally harmless, while others leak toxic metals when their glaze dissolves and can seriously harm fish.

If you are uncertain of a ceramic ornament's safety, water down some vinegar to a pH close to the most acidic conditions your aquarium will encounter. Only a pH of 5 should be enough. Immerse the ornament in this solution and wait a month before re-examining. Take a look at the glaze. If the object's shininess has degraded, this suggests chemical leaking and that the object is unfit for aquatic use. Unglazed ceramics such as terracotta are ideal because they do not pose any possibility of chemical leakage. Ceramics with sharp edges can be chipped away to avoid damage and covered in a ring of marine silicone.

x.   Aquarium Stones and Rocks

Many attractive stones, pebbles, and rocks serve as perfect additions to many aquariums. Naturally themed ponds comfort the fish by imitating their native environment. You can also attach rocks to your aquarium as well. However, before doing so, it is vital that you boil the rocks for an hour before adding them to prevent toxic substances/organisms from being brought in. Be conscious too, certain rocks such as lace rock can be sharp and hurt your fish, and should be avoided. Glass rock, ice rock, river pebbles, zebra rock and rainbow rock are all appealing options.

xi.   Bubble Makers

Not only do bubble tops, underwater rivers and air stones look enticing, but they are also a critical addition to densely populated aquariums. If you have one or more highly active fish in a single tank, it is necessary to make sure they have a sufficient oxygen supply. Livelier fish can consume more than sluggish species, so it's important to keep the oxygen levels high by adding decorations that generate air. Make sure they aren't too big for your fish to handle when introducing bubble makers into your aquarium. If the water flow is too strong, fish may find it hard to swim, and it could also lead to illness.

It's important to incorporate decorations and accessories into any decor to make them eye catching as well as safe and non-toxic. The bright colors or odd decorations you may want to add to your fish are indifferent. You can add your favorite ornaments to your aquarium without thinking about hurting your fish by using the tips above.

Things you shouldn't put in your fish tank

If you put some objects in your aquarium unknowingly, you could very well endanger your fish, and worse yet some products could be fatal.

1) Plastic

Most fish shops sell plastic toys to use in your fish tank, like Nemo or SpongeBob. If plastics are left in water for a long time, they can release potentially harmful chemicals into the water so they should be avoided at all costs in fish tanks. If the plastic has been marked food safe, there are a range of exceptions to this. This is also illustrated with three arrows forming a triangle.

The plastic toys that you can buy from the fish stores are always painted, and the paints may not have been sealed. If purchasing plastic toys, make sure you find out whether they have been tested and are suitable for your aquarium. Unsealed, painted plastic toys can release toxins that may kill your fish. Even with sealed plastic, they are likely to chip or break, and then release contaminants into the water.

2) Ceramics that are not dinner safe

Many ceramics are OK to use in your tank as long as they are labeled as 'dinnerware protected'. A simple rule of thumb for ceramics is, don't place it in your aquarium because it is not safe to feed with. There are a few exceptions to this rule.

There is also evidence that lead is found in some pottery, which is both a threat to humans and fish alike. Often highly decorated products and glazed terra cotta clay can contain lead, but for years now, most countries have been producing lead free terracotta.

3) Anything consumable

No other consumables should be put in your tank besides the food you provide for your fish. Fish can only chew so much, and if you put loose rock in the tank, even a small piece could be fatal. Be sure that you know all the side effects of introducing stuff to your tank. Even some plants are toxic to fish, so do your homework thoroughly.

4) Untreated wood

Most wooden ornaments in pet shops that you find for fish tanks are typically safe to buy, but you should always ask an attendant to explain the risks of having wooden ornaments in your fish tank. If driftwood is to be used, you should select a hard wood. This is because it takes a long time for hard woods to decompose and would have no immediate effects on the water.

5) Untreated beach sand

Although treated sand can make a great substratum, beach sand is usually polluted and contains chemical residues that can harm your fish. You can put sand in your fish tanks, but make sure it's aquarium safe. If you're willing to use beach sand in your tank, be aware that it soaks up the sand and slightly adjusts the temperature in the tank.

6) Avoid anything sharp

It goes without saying, but don't put anything sharp inside your fish tank. That includes glass with jagged edges, painted glass, sharp edged objects or other decorations with sharp edges. Paint can make objects flake off and poison your fish.

7) Large fish breeds

This may be common sense to those more seasoned aquarists, but it's something that needs to be discussed. If you have a 100-gallon aquarium, there are still a lot of fish types that aren't suitable for your fish tank. One example is the Iridescent Shark, a big Catfish-like species that is an extreme swimmer and can expand in the wild for up to 4 feet long. Please be mindful of the types of fish you add to your tank. Adding the wrong fish will not only be a waste of money, but will prove to be a risk to other smaller fish in your tank.

8) Degradable items

If you put something in your tank that might be degradable, it will tamper with the water in your aquarium. It can also release pollutants and chemicals in the water depending on the product, and it can also make the water dirty. It's worth noting that fish food should be left in the aquarium for only five minutes, and the rest should be discarded to minimize the amount of waste left in the tank.

9) Your hands

Putting your hands inside your fish tank is okay as long as they are not dirty. And by this, we mean that hand cleaning products and creams should be washed off thoroughly. Cleaning products and other contaminants left on your hands can be toxic to your fish. Before sticking your hands in the tank, wash them with soap and rinse

114

them off thoroughly to make sure the soap is completely removed.

10) Shells and corals in freshwater aquariums
Shells and corals contribute calcium to the fish tank, and freshwater tanks don't need that. Basically, nothing should be placed in the tank that causes chemical changes in the water. Seashells for example change the hardness of a pH level, which will cause difficulties for your fish, and will create more challenges to maintain the tank.

18. WHAT YOU NEED TO KNOW ABOUT WATER TEST KITS

Checking aquarium water is a vital component of keeping the fish safe. Perfect water quality and poor water quality can look identical in an aquarium system. Let say the water in your tank has high levels of ammonia. The challenge is you can't possibly see it with the naked eye. The difference to your fish however, is clear. It is painfully obvious. Since poor water quality can cause stress to your fish, and can also lead to sickness and even death, it is something you want to track closely.

So, how can you search for what your eyes are unable to see? This is where an aquarium test kit comes in play to test your aquarium water quality.

A test kit for aquariums is designed to calculate a particular parameter for water. The reason why a test kit is so necessary is that a parameter mismatch in the water will cause havoc in your tank. Consider nitrites. For example, if your tank levels rise too high, your fish will die. By continuously monitoring the water with a test kit, you ensure that the water parameters are within acceptable limits.

The following is a list of items you will find in a typical test kit:

- ❖ Instructions
- ❖ Test tube
- ❖ Testing solution
- ❖ Color card

The test tube comes with both aquarium water and a few drops of the test solution. Wait for the color change solution and compare it with the color card to obtain a result. Although it might not look like much, this simple little kit is your frontline protection in the fight for high water quality. It doesn't matter whether you are a novice or an expert; a test kit is an essential piece of equipment for aquariums.

You should remember that a test kit can only evaluate a single water parameter. For each water parameter you wish to verify, you need to buy a test kit. Many parameters can be tested in fish tanks including nitrates, PH, oxygen, copper, etc.

Fortunately you're not going to need any of those. The exact parameter that you will need to check for will rely solely on your tank system. In fact, you only need a few test kits to get started if you are a novice: ammonia, nitrite, nitrate and pH, and probably KH, depending on your source of water. Each test for an aquarium that the average beginner requires comes in a simple, compact, and inexpensive pack.

Extra parameters to test for in aquariums

1) **Copper** - Most tap water could contain high levels of copper, especially in installations that use copper pipes. Fish differ in exposure to copper, and copper is absorbed from the water by the fish and retained in their bodies so that copper can have a cumulative effect and become poisonous to fish, which also has a low copper content. When copper containing medicine is used to treat sick fish, copper tests are needed. Copper testing allows the correct dosage of the aquarium water when copper treatments are provided.

2) **Oxygen -** Densely occupied tanks such as those that breeders may have or densely planted tanks are two cases where oxygen levels will need to be examined more closely.

3) **Hardness and Alkalinity** - The hardness is also referred to as General Hardness (GH) & alkalinity can be referred to as Carbonate Hardness (KH). Hardness (GH) tests whether the water is soft or hard. GH should be matched to the species of fish being housed. Tetras, for example, perform well in softer water while most African cichlids thrive in hard water. GH is particularly important when fish are breeding.

Alkalinity (KH) has a significant effect on the stability of the pH. It affects the fish species that will survive in the tank, apart from being critical for the beneficial bacteria in the biofilter that purify the waste, rendering it an important metric for periodic evaluation. The higher the KH, the more stable the pH is.

4) **Phosphate** - Generally, phosphate is used in salt water aquariums to promote algae growth. Phosphate is not a widely used freshwater aquarium check since elevated levels do not affect the fish. Knowing the phosphate level will help to decide whether the steps being taken to reduce the levels of phosphate are having the desired effect while fighting algae problems. Phosphate can be introduced by fish feeds into the tank, as well as through the local tap water.

5) **Iron** - Plants require iron to survive, and those who maintain heavily planted tanks or propagate plants may measure the level of commercial iron supplements for planted aquariums. The iron test kits can help decide how much to apply to the aquarium. If you find high phosphate in the aquarium, changes in water will help, unless your local tap water is high in phosphate too. Make sure to check the water in the tank, or contact the local water provider to see if phosphate is in the drinking water.

6) **Calcium -** Calcium deposition produces dry, crusty looking spots and stains on an aquarium's interior, around the sides, at the hood's bottom, and even on the filter. Naturally, calcium is present in water so that calcium accumulation won't hurt your fish. When it appears in your tank, it is just aesthetically unattractive.

How to use a test kit for your aquarium

1) Filling the test tube
Get some water from your aquarium into a test tube. Use a disposable pipette to transfer the water into the tube to avoid contamination of the sample.

2) Add your testing solution
Then take the test solution and add three droplets to the test tube. As drops are added, a colored cloud may begin to form in the water. Verify that the test product has not expired. The use of an outdated test kit could pose problems with accuracy. Luckily, test kits have usually a long shelf life.

3) Shake the mixture
Give a light shake to the test tube. Doing this would ensure the test solution has mixed equally with the water. The mixture inside the test tube will now be a single even color.

4) Match the test sample in the tube to the color card
All that remains to do now is match the color of your test tube to the color chart that comes with the package. The outcome is whichever color is nearest.

How often should an aquarium test kit be used?
You can check your water every day when you first cycle your aquarium so that you can keep an eye on how your new tank progresses through the nitrogen cycle. After your tank has been set up and cycled, and a good maintenance routine has been established, you can drop the test down to once a week. If you note any issues in

your aquarium, such as stressed fish or cloudy water, check immediately, you may find that the problem is probably caused by a single water parameter.

Accuracy of test kits

- Test strips are the least accurate
- Test kits are Accurate
- Scientific meters and probes are precise

Although they may not be as precise as scientific meters, aquarium test kits are probably the best way to test your aquarium parameters, at least for beginners and those who view it as a casual hobby. The principal explanation for their success is that they're cheap.

Things to consider when buying aquarium test kits

- Ease of use
- Accuracy
- Type of water in your aquarium
- Shelf life

Benefits of test kits

- **Analyzes ammonia** - High levels of ammonia in the fish tank can be toxic to the fish. This shows us that ammonia levels should be closely monitored in the fish tank in order to keep the fish healthy and safe.

- **Checks algae growth** - Checking the phosphate levels in the aquarium to make sure the water doesn't turn mist green due to algae blooms in the water. When you see that the tank water appears greenish and misty, then the probable cause is the building up of algae.

- **Promotes coral growth** - Healthy calcium levels in the water encourage coral growth, but too much of it stains the fish tank.

- **Determines pH** - The pH (acid based solution balance) is a key parameter for all aquariums and should be continuously checked and reported in a log. Dramatic pH changes also constitute the unseen cause of fish disease and death. Gradual changes in pH are less extreme in the short term but can eventually be just as harmful to fish health as a sudden shift in pH.

- **Checks for chlorine levels -** Tap water contains chlorine levels that are safe for human consumption but not for fish. Testing for Chlorine ensures the fish stay alive. Chlorine levels in fish tanks should be 0.

19. CHOOSING THE BEST FOOD FOR YOUR FISH

Aquarium fish's nutritional requirements differ considerably depending on species, as well as age. Choosing the right fish food for aquariums is key to maintaining healthy fish. Adequate dietary quality along with predetermined fish feeding times and habits are very important. Keep in mind that nocturnal fish, day dwellers, top feeders, bottom feeders etc. require special attention. Offering a variety of pellets that float and sink should be a staple in any community tank.

Choosing good food for the fish

An inexperienced owner could consider the fish food section at the pet store overwhelming. Second, learn more about your fish species, starting with whether the species is an eater of meat (carnivores) or eater of vegetation (herbivores).

Types of fish

There are hundreds of Aquarium Fish species. To choose the right food that will aid in the health and longevity of your fish, it is crucial to know whether the fish are plant eaters, meat eaters or omnivorous (eat both plant and animal).

- Carnivores (meat eaters): Acara, Archerfish, Bettas and Oscar
- Herbivores (plants, algae and fruit eaters): Molly, Farowella, Pacu and Tropheus
- Omnivores (meat and vegetables eaters): Goldfish, Danios and Loaches.

Different tank feeding levels for fish:

- Surface feeders
- Mid-water feeders
- Bottom feeders

Most fish will learn to eat anywhere they can, but timid fish will wait until food drips into their "safe zone." Such fish will need to be fed as targets, which ensures that food is directed right to them. Usually, flakes and some pellet foods remain on the surface for a minute or two before a gradual descent to the bottom begins, making them an excellent choice for surface and midwater feeding. Soaking dried food or "swishing" it on the surface can make them drop faster for feeders from mid-water. Sinking sticks, wafers and pellet foods, most catfish, loaches and other bottom feeders perform pretty well.

When should you feed your fish?

The majority of fish eat early in the morning and at dusk. Exceptions are herbivores and omnivores, and nocturnal animals who forage all day long. While aquarium fish can be fed at any time of day, feedings are best for both morning and evening. They easily learn to swim back and forth in the water or emerge from hiding places in anticipation of their next meal, when "food time" is around.

Try to ensure that the aquarium light is on for at least 30 minutes before feeding in the morning and keep it on for at least 30 minutes after feeding in the evening. Nocturnal species such as knife fish, catfish and some plecostomus may be fed food shortly after the light of the aquarium is turned off when night comes.

Different Forms of Fish Food

- **Flake Foods** - Flake food is among the most common food type used to feed tropical fish. It is ideal for medium to small fish, including breeds of the general population such as livebearers, barbs, and tetras. Many farmers grow flake products, so you have a wide variety to choose from. Choosing fish flake food from some reputable manufacturers would be best. One that comes to mind is the Omega One Super Color Flakes in a 2.2 oz size. Try to provide a variety of different types and brands of flakes, and other types of fish food.

- **Pellet and Granular Foods** - There are also common types of micro pellets and granulated fish foods to choose from. These are a great alternative to flake food, and thus help to offer a diverse diet for your fish. These foods sink easily through the mud and are therefore ideal for bottom or midwater fish feeding. Pellet and granular foods are also a great choice for auto feeders too.

- **Freeze-Dried Foods** - Freeze-dried foods allow you to feed your fish with naturally occurring foods such as bloodworms and tubifex that are healthier for them than live foods, and generally better than frozen food. Foods such as frozen bloodworms can float, making them a wonderful choice for those fish that feed near the water, such as African butterfly fish, hatchet fish and gouramis. Freeze-dried tubifex is created in a cube-shaped form that can be pushed against the wall of your aquarium to help your fish feed in full view. You can include Tubifex worms and Mysis shrimp or other foods as freeze-dried cubes. They are perfect for carnivorous fish and are very nutritious as well.

- **Tablet and Wafer Food** - Tablet and large wafer disks are ideal for bottom fed fish. They drop quickly through the water and are usually too big for the smaller fish to swallow entirely, allowing them to be fed by bottom feed fish such as loaches and catfish. Such foods are also ideal for various catfish suckermouth that pick at the surfaces of the food. Tablet and wafer food allow these fish to take their food in small quantities over a more extended period, much as they would take their food in their natural environment. Many types of tablet food can be placed against the glass wall of your tank so that the fish can see it clearly and feed on it.

- **Frozen Foods** -The pet store's freezer department houses a large assortment of frozen treats. Starting with frozen shrimp, bloodworms, plankton, prawn, krill, musts, etc. They usually come in variety packs. Veggies and spirulina also come in freezer packs. The pre-portioned cubes usually dissolve first, making it easier for feeding.

- **Vegetable Foods** - Diverse household vegetables can be used in your tank to feed the omnivorous & herbivores. Many fish keepers give veggies like cucumbesr and cabbage to the Suckermouth catfish. This can be kept overnight in the tank, so

126

the fish can nibble on them. They should however be removed the following morning.

- **Live Foods** - While live foods are not so common nowadays, due to the availability of so many types of healthy fish foods, many fish owners prefer to feed them as occasional treats. It may also be a good option for some wild fish, which takes time to get used to aquarium foods.

- **Fry Foods** - For those fish that don't eat readily prepared foods, live foods are a perfect choice. Furthermore, if you have to feed a large number of fish, this will be a great option. Microworms and baby brine shrimp are the two species most popularly cultivated for this purpose. You can feed them a few times a day, but note that you'll need to change the water more frequently.

- **Sticks and Floating Pellets** - Like other cichlids, floating pellets and larger food sticks are suitable for big fish. Such foods serve as a healthy diet that won't get lost as quickly as finer foods in the intake part of the filter. Many farmers make pellets and sticks for carnivores or herbivores. As for omnivores, each of these food types can be rotated.

Tips to feed fish in aquariums

In the oceans, lakes and rivers, fish can feed whenever they are hungry as food is always available. This means they are eating several times a day, or they may not be feeding at a time for several days. It's best to stick to a daily schedule for feeding your fish in your home aquarium, make sure to choose the diet that's appropriate for the type of fish you have in your tank.

- Know what sort of diet your fish needs. Do some basic research to find out what kind of food the fish wants and the best way to deliver it.

- Feed your fish twice a day, no more. Most fish do well with a single daily feeding, but some herbivorous fish such as mollies and silver dollars need to snack.

- When you have nocturnal fish in your tank, note when you feed them, because it's best to feed them right before the light goes out for the night.
- Give the fish food that they can eat for only five minutes. Over feeding the fish means much of the food ends up falling to the bottom of the tank, where it decomposes and reduces the consistency of the water in the tank.

- Adhere to a healthy staple diet for your fish (such as a healthy herbivorous pellet for herbivores) and supplement it several times a week with limited amounts of fresh food.

- When feeding fresh foods and dissolving food forms (like algae wafers), remove the unleavened (type of bread) part after 30 to 60 minutes, so it does not dirty the tank.

- Note, the more you feed your fish, the more it creates waste. Waste can decompose rapidly in an enclosed setting such as your fish tank, so make sure to keep the conditions in your tank clean and stable.

- It is important to note that most fish eat small amounts at a time particularly when compared to larger pets such as cats and dogs.

- Stop purchasing fish food in bulk because it is unlikely you can consume it all before it begins to lose its nutritional value. Buy small quantities and keep them fresh, so that your fish get the full value from what you give them.

Advantages and drawbacks of buying fish food online

PROS

- One key benefit is that you can find all kinds of fish food online. You're not limited to what is in stock at your local pet shop. You can buy any form of food, including freeze-dried fish meals or flakes, and it's normally available in any size.

- Online reviews from reputable websites and fish keeping blogs are helpful when it comes to what buyers are saying about a particular fish food, and the experiences they are having with those products.

- In some cases, when you buy in bulk, you will get discounts when you shop online.

CONS

- Most novices don't really like online shopping for fish food as they have to wait for delivery, and often shipping comes with a fee.

- The time spent researching and reviewing fish food products can be overwhelming.

COMMON INGREDIENTS IN FISH FOOD

You should be familiar with some of the ingredients in fish foods. Take the time to read the label to familiarize yourself with the nutritional value of the various foods. Here are some of the ingredients which you might find:

- Fish Meal – One of the primary ingredients in most carnivore foods, fish meal, is a quality source of aquatic animal protein.

- Spirulina – Spirulina is also known as blue green algae and is a common ingredient in herbivorous foods. This is a healthy source of plant protein, as well as vitamin B12 and amino acids.

- Whole Fish – there's not much difference between fish mean and whole fish other than when it can be used.

- Algae Meal – A dried product made from blue green algae, algae meal is a good source of amino acids, vitamins, and trace elements, but not as good as spirulina.

- Krill – Small shrimp-like crustaceans and an excellent source of protein, amino acids, and omega 3 fatty acids which are a popular ingredient in carnivorous foods.

- Brewer's Dried Yeast – This ingredient contains about 45 percent protein and is high in vitamin B but is not the best protein source for fish.

- Wheat Germ – Wheat germ is extracted from the wheat berry and other parts of wheat and is rich in nutrients and easily digestible to humans.

- Corn Gluten Meal – A plant-based protein extracted from maize. Maize gluten meal is not a favored ingredient because it is not as digestible as other proteins, but is sometimes used as a filler ingredient.

- Rice Bran – This ingredient forms the majority of rice's nutrient content and is a good source of digestible fiber for fish.

Problems that can arise from overfeeding fish

Overfeeding is the primary cause of death for fish. Overfeeding results in the accumulation of waste due to uneaten food and increased amounts of waste created by fish consuming more than they actually need. Fish are very easy to overfeed. First of all, we forget how small they are: our appetites are far greater than their bellies. Secondly, feeding is one of the few ways we can communicate with our fish, so we try to do it too often. Thirdly, fish know quickly that our behavior always means food is on the way. They arrive at the front and top of the tank and look hungry and eager. We need to be careful about overfeeding. Here are some of the dangers of overfeeding fish and what to look out for:

- High ammonia and nitrites - Protein is broken down into ammonia and nitrites in unfed food and fish waste, which are highly harmful to fish.

- Low oxygen levels - It is an aerobic process, meaning that it uses oxygen and creates carbon dioxide, which ensures less dissolved oxygen is present in the tank or pond for use by the fish.

- Low pH levels - Low pH levels is the breakdown of organic material that lowers the amount of oxygen, the pH of the water is also lowered because acids are released during the process. Every fish species has an optimum pH range, even as the breakdown of organic material decreases the amount of oxygen, it also decreases the pH of the water since acids are formed during the process.

- Fin rot - Fin rot is a disease in which a moth-eaten, shaggy appearance may grow on the fins. This typically happens when fish are overfed.

- Fatty liver - Fatty liver, or hepatic lipidosis, is a condition that occurs more often in African cichlids and rainbowfish. It affects liver function, which can contribute to the fish's death.

- Improper digestion - The amount and type of food in ponds need to be changed as the weather gets colder. You should feed wheat germ based food exclusively to your koi below 60 ° F, and because bacterial processes slow down, the amount fed should be reduced. The bacteria in the digestive system of a fish can no longer absorb food below 50 ° F.

- Algae bloom - The growth of algae is one of the most common problems seen in aquariums. Unsightly blue-green and red algae multiply when the water contains significant amounts of dissolved organic content, nitrates, and phosphates, which are common occurrences with overfed fish.

- Clogged filters - Filter systems are designed to eliminate the usual amount of waste materials that form over time due to overfeeding. It becomes evident on filters, when you see uneaten food and waste materials accumulating.

- Mold – when gravel, plants, and other decorations have white, cotton like material that grows on them, mold or fungus may be the problem. Just like algae, these species expand as the levels of organic matter in the water are increased.

20. HOW AQUARIUM CHILLERS WORK

What is an Aquarium chiller? An aquarium chiller chills the water in a fish tank and makes it possible to keep species that need a lower water temperature. Most aquarium chillers use a form of vapor compression to chill the water in your aquarium. Although the science behind this method can be a little complicated, knowing the basic concepts and components to operate and maintain the chiller properly is a good idea. The aquarium chiller is fitted with a thermostat control unit much like a heater to allow you to set the optimal temperature for your particular aquarium.

If the ambient room temperature is higher than the ideal water temperature, you need an aquarium chiller. This may be one of many causes:

- You live in a warm climate part of the world, and it's not a choice to decrease your temperature indoors low enough.

- You live in an environment that is subject to seasonal heat spells that raise room temperatures and unexpectedly cause havoc in your aquarium.

- You installed heat emitting equipment that raises the temperature of the water, such as pumps and lights.

Under no circumstance should aquariums get hotter than 83° F. The oxygen level in aquarium water begins to decrease at 83° F or a higher water temperature, and this leads to a stressful situation for the fish to receive oxygen. Be cautious as this may lead to sickness or death of your fish in the aquarium. It is recommended to keep them in a safe water temperature for optimum protection. Tropical fish and saltwater aquarium fish, for example have an acceptable range of 72° to 80° F (optimal 78° F), and Fancy Tail Goldfish has an acceptable range of 65° to 72° F and Common Goldfish also has an acceptable range of 65° to 68° F.

You should not keep your aquariums in a position where the sun is in direct contact. This would lead to a rise in algae growth which would be hard to clean. In many instances, placing the chiller inside the aquarium cabinet is probably not a good idea. The heat that the chiller has drained from the tank is poured into the sealed refrigerator, and could possibly reheat the tank.

To extract heat from the refrigerant, the chiller uses a ventilator to blow air over the heated condenser coil. Aquarium chillers should be installed in an environment with ample ventilation to hold the heat exiting from the aquarium and chiller. If the chiller is unable to release the heat, it is less effective and wastes energy.

HOW DO AQUARIUM CHILLERS WORK?

An aquarium chiller works by extracting the heat from the water and then moving it to another location within the unit. This process is also called the exchange of heat. The chiller has a heat exchanger, expansion valve, compressor, and condenser coil parts.

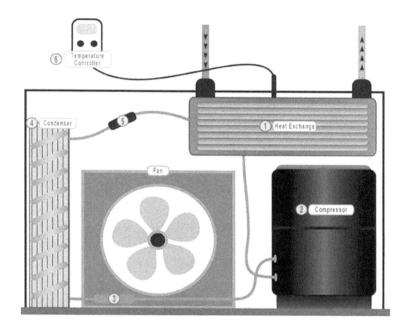

The diagram above describes the basic parts found on popular aquarium chillers, and we have outlined the various functions below to help you understand how an aquarium chiller operates.

I. Water from the aquarium is pumped into the chiller and goes into the heat exchanger. Aquarium water flows inside the heat exchanger through a series of cold, refrigerant filled metal coils. It is here that heat is transferred into the refrigerant from your aquarium water.

II. Heated coolant is compressed, and inside the pump, it transforms from a liquid into a

137

gas. What pushes the refrigerant through the cooling system is the pressure generated within the compressor.

III. Gaseous refrigerant is sent from the compressor to the condenser. A ventilator blasts air over the condenser, cooling the refrigerant inside and releasing heat around the chiller to the atmosphere. This is why the location of your chiller should be in a well ventilated area.

IV. The refrigerant is then cooled and condensed back into a liquid by passing through the condenser.

V. The condensed refrigerant passes through an expansion valve, which reduces the pressure inside the refrigerant line controlling the rate at which the aquarium water is cooled inside the evaporator or heat exchanger.

VI. The temperature monitor controls the temperature of your aquarium water and turns the chiller ON automatically as the temperature increases, turning it OFF when the temperature is below the correct range. The temperature controller is built into most chillers but sometimes sold separately depending on the brand of the chiller.

Tips for aquarium chillers

- Do not unplug the aquarium heater when a chiller is in use because an unplugged heater may cause a severe temperature drop.

- Do not enclose the chiller or place it inside aquarium furniture unless the furniture is very well ventilated. This is because the chiller itself emits heat that can be transmitted into the aquarium.

- Pick a chiller that does not produce excess noise as it may cause a disturbance.

- Never allow your chiller to run dry; this can cause damage to internal components.

- Chillers use a significant amount of power; in addition to all the other equipment on your aquarium, be sure to account for the required electricity use.

- Inside the heat exchanger, calcium build up can reduce the chilling efficiency; daily back-flushing with a freshwater/vinegar solution can help to eliminate build-up, and keep your chiller running at optimum efficiency.

- Use LED lighting for your aquariums because LEDs produce less heat than other forms of lighting.

Final Thoughts

While taking care of fish might seem like a daunting task to the novice aquarist, practice often makes the process of keeping fish much easier. Consider each fish's specific needs and ensure that you do your part to keep them alive. After a few weeks into the hobby, you might decide to add more fish or buy a larger aquarium as your hobby grows.

Enjoy your aquarium!

Printed in the USA
CPSIA information can be obtained
at www.ICGtesting.com
LVHW052155010524
779100LV00033B/1136

9 798670 988070